Living God's Word

Living God's Word

Reflections on the Sunday Readings for Year C

Archbishop Terrence Prendergast

NOVALIS

© 2012 Novalis Publishing Inc.

Cover design and layout: Audrey Wells

Cover art: "Evangelista Luca" - mosaico realizzato dalla Scuola Mosaicisti del Friuli (Spilimbergo PN - Italia), a.s. 1960/1961, bozzetto di Padre Leo Coppens ["Luke the Evangelist," Mosaic created by The School of Mosaic of Friuli (Spilimbergo, PN - Italy), 1960/1961, sketch by Fr. Leo Coppens.]

Published by Novalis

Publishing Office
10 Lower Spadina Avenue, Suite 400
Toronto, Ontario, Canada
M5V 2Z2

Head Office
4475 Frontenac Street
Montréal, Québec, Canada
H2H 2S2

www.novalis.ca

Cataloguing in Publication is available from Library and Archives Canada.

Printed in Canada.

The lectionary texts contained herein are from the *Lectionary, Sundays and Solemnities* of the Canadian Conference of Catholic Bishops, Copyright © Concacan Inc., 1992, 2009. All rights reserved. Used by permission of the Canadian Conference of Catholic Bishops.

This revised edition of the *Lectionary, Sundays and Solemnities* follows the *Ordo Lectionum Missae, editio typica altera*, Typis Polyglottis Vaticanus, 1981.

The Scripture quotations contained herein (including the texts of the readings, the Psalms, the Psalm refrains and the Gospel verses) are based on the New Revised Standard Version of the Bible, copyright © 1989 National Council of the Churches of Christ in the USA. Adapted and used by permission. All rights reserved.

Adaptations for liturgical use have been made to selected Scripture texts. These adaptations have been made to bring the readings into conformity with the *Ordo Lectionum Missae, editio typica altera*, the *Lectionarium* and *Liturgiam Authenticam*, as well as to facilitate proclamation. These adaptations were prepared by and are the sole responsibility of the Canadian Conference of Catholic Bishops. Adaptations copyright © 2009 National Council of the Churches of Christ in the USA. Used by permission. All rights reserved.

All rights reserved. No part of this publication may be reproduced, stored in a retrieval system, or transmitted in any form, or by any means, electronic, mechanical, photocopying, recording, or otherwise, without the written permission of the publisher.

We acknowledge the financial support of the Government of Canada through the Canada Book Fund for business development activities.

5   4   3   2   1   16   15   14   13   12

Dedication

To MY BROTHER PRIESTS

"The greatest among you must become like the youngest,
and the leader like one who serves ...
I am among you as one who serves ..."

(Luke 22.26-27)

Acknowledgements

Over a ten-year period, it was my privilege to write a weekly set of reflections on the Sunday readings ("God's Word on Sunday") in the Toronto-based newspaper *The Catholic Register*.

On several occasions, friends and associates suggested that these be made available in book form as an aid to those who have the challenge of providing homiletical reflections for parish and other faith communities. I have also been told that liturgy committees and study groups that gather to pray over the Scriptures in preparation for their participation in the Sunday Eucharist appreciate these reflections.

Joseph Sinasac of Novalis, who was my editor at the *Register*, prodded me to select the best of my earlier work and to write new reflections to cover any gaps in the columns caused either by an early start to Lent or by the late resumption of continuous readings after Pentecost. I am grateful for his encouragement and his patience.

My thanks go, too, to Anne Louise Mahoney, whose competent, efficient and speedy work in copy editing brought consistency, harmony and clarity to a text that had gestated over a number of years.

The present collection of readings from the liturgical year of Luke (designated "Year C" in lectionaries) has been supplemented with a brief treatment of *Lectio divina* (a type of holy reading) to take up the image of Jesus as one who prays and teaches his disciples how to pray.

As I commend this aid to Sunday worship to disciples aspiring to deepen their knowledge and love of the Scriptures, I am conscious of my own debt to teachers and ministers of the word who have helped me: several Jesuit confreres have assisted me immensely, as have scholar friends in the Catholic Biblical Association of America, whose annual convention was always a joy, and the scholarly communities where I spent refreshing sabbatical years: the Pontifical Biblical Institute in Rome (1987–88) and the École biblique in Jerusalem (1994–1995). May these associates rejoice in seeing ideas and expressions I have gleaned from their academic labours being handed on. Any inadequacy in transmitting their research remains entirely my own responsibility.

This work is dedicated in homage to the priests who have guided, challenged and encouraged me – those who, by a godly life and zeal in ministry, have taught me to strive to be an *alter Christus* in the post-conciliar time of transition – on this day on which I observe the 40th anniversary of my priestly ordination.

+Terrence Prendergast, S.J.
Archbishop of Ottawa
The Solemnity of the Most Holy Body and Blood of Christ
June 10, 2012

Contents

Foreword by Thomas Cardinal Collins 10
Introduction 13

First Sunday of Advent 20
Second Sunday of Advent 22
Third Sunday of Advent 24
Fourth Sunday of Advent 26
The Holy Family of Jesus, Mary and Joseph 29
Epiphany of the Lord 31
The Baptism of the Lord 33
Second Sunday in Ordinary Time 36
Third Sunday in Ordinary Time 38
Fourth Sunday in Ordinary Time 40
Fifth Sunday in Ordinary Time 43
Sixth Sunday in Ordinary Time 45
Seventh Sunday in Ordinary Time 47
First Sunday of Lent 50
Second Sunday of Lent 52
Third Sunday of Lent 54
Fourth Sunday of Lent 57
Fifth Sunday of Lent 59
Palm Sunday of the Lord's Passion 61
The Resurrection of the Lord: Easter Sunday 64
Second Sunday of Easter 66
Third Sunday of Easter 68
Fourth Sunday of Easter 70

Fifth Sunday of Easter	73
Sixth Sunday of Easter	75
Ascension of the Lord	77
Seventh Sunday of Easter	80
The Solemnity of Pentecost	82
The Most Holy Trinity	84
The Most Holy Body and Blood of Christ	87
Eighth Sunday in Ordinary Time	89
Ninth Sunday in Ordinary Time	92
Tenth Sunday in Ordinary Time	94
Eleventh Sunday in Ordinary Time	96
Twelfth Sunday in Ordinary Time	99
Thirteenth Sunday in Ordinary Time	101
Fourteenth Sunday in Ordinary Time	103
Fifteenth Sunday in Ordinary Time	106
Sixteenth Sunday in Ordinary Time	108
Seventeenth Sunday in Ordinary Time	110
Eighteenth Sunday in Ordinary Time	112
Nineteenth Sunday in Ordinary Time	115
Twentieth Sunday in Ordinary Time	117
Twenty-first Sunday in Ordinary Time	119
Twenty-second Sunday in Ordinary Time	122
Twenty-third Sunday in Ordinary Time	124
Twenty-fourth Sunday in Ordinary Time	126
Twenty-fifth Sunday in Ordinary Time	128
Twenty-sixth Sunday in Ordinary Time	131
Twenty-seventh Sunday in Ordinary Time	133
Twenty-eighth Sunday in Ordinary Time	135
Twenty-ninth Sunday in Ordinary Time	138
Thirtieth Sunday in Ordinary Time	140
Thirty-first Sunday in Ordinary Time	143
Thirty-second Sunday in Ordinary Time	145
Thirty-third Sunday in Ordinary Time	147
Thirty-fourth Sunday in Ordinary Time (Christ the King)	150

Foreword

From the earliest days of the Church, Christians have gathered each Sunday, on the day of the Resurrection, to celebrate the holy sacrifice of the Mass. As a fundamental part of that liturgy, we listen to the inspired words of Scripture, which give light for the path ahead in the coming week. Already in the Gospel of Luke, in the account of the disciples on the road to Emmaus, we hear how their hearts burned within them as Jesus spoke to them of the sacred Scriptures, before they finally came to recognize him in the breaking of the bread.

Jesus himself is the Word of God, but we encounter him in the Eucharistic liturgy in word and sacrament. The first part of the Mass, the Liturgy of the Word, is a precious way not only of gaining holy wisdom to guide us, but also of encountering Jesus personally through the inspired text, as we prepare to encounter him personally through the Holy Eucharist in the second part of the Mass.

The Bible, especially the New Testament, has its natural home in the celebration of the Eucharist; this is the privileged setting in which we listen to the words of life in the midst of the community of disciples, in the context of the sacrament of the Eucharist, and with the benefit of the homily. The words of the homily help us to come to a deeper appreciation of the meaning of the sacred text in relation to our whole faith, and to apply it to our own lives, so that we might live in accord with it as we move from the Mass to our daily service of our Lord.

But often the Liturgy of the Word does not have that effect. We hurry to Mass, and no sooner has the first reading been completed than we forget what it says, and so with each of the readings. They come at us quickly, and sometimes we have the practical problem of not being able to hear them properly. Although those who designed the Sunday Lectionary followed a careful plan, with a different Gospel highlighted each year over a three-year cycle, and with the first reading, from the Old Testament, chosen to shed light on the Gospel, each reading is a very small piece of the Bible, taken out of the context of the book in which it is found. So the Sunday Eucharist, the most important setting for our experience of the Bible, can become a place in which the Words of Life go in one ear and out the other. That is not acceptable, especially as we need to be deeply transformed by both word and sacrament at the Sunday Eucharist, so that we can properly fulfill our mission to evangelize this increasingly secular society.

If anything is worthwhile, we need to prepare for it properly, and that is surely true of the Liturgy of the Word, as it is also true for the Liturgy of the Eucharist. When we care, we prepare.

In this volume, *Living God's Word*, on Year C of the Lectionary, in which we primarily reflect on the Gospel of Luke, Archbishop Prendergast (as he does in the accompanying volumes for Year A and Year B) offers us most valuable assistance in preparing to listen with heart and mind to God's voice in the Liturgy of the Word. He is a renowned scripture scholar, and provides the background information that helps us to appreciate the meaning of the Sunday readings; as well, he offers insights based on his experience as a disciple and successor of the apostles. It is most fitting that when a bishop is ordained, the Book of the Gospels is held open over his head as the prayer of consecration is said, for it is his mission to serve in the imitation of Christ on the road to Emmaus, helping the disciples of the Lord to become ignited with the fire of God's Word so that they can evangelize the society into which they are sent back at the end of the Eucharist.

May this book help those who are preparing to preach, and all who are preparing attentively to listen to God's Word at the Sunday Eucharist, so that they may faithfully fulfill the mission they have received.

Thomas Cardinal Collins
Archbishop of Toronto

Introduction

I. The Year of Luke

Every year, in late November or early December, the Church begins the celebration of a new liturgical year. The scriptural readings are part of a three-year cycle. In Year C, the gospel readings are drawn chiefly from Luke's Gospel. Several Sundays after Christmas, during Lent and in Eastertide are taken from the Gospel of John; this also happens in Year A, which is devoted mainly to Matthew's Gospel, and in Year B, when selections are taken primarily from the Gospel of Mark.

This book offers reflections on the Sundays of Year C. Reflections on the Solemnities of Our Lord, the Blessed Virgin Mary and other important feasts of saints, of all the faithful departed, and of the dedication of the Basilica Cathedral of St. John Lateran – which can displace the Sunday celebration in Ordinary Time – are found in *Living God's Word: Reflections on the Sunday Readings for Year A* (Novalis, 2010).

Generally speaking, the first reading, which is from the Old Testament (except in Eastertide, when selections from the Acts of the Apostles are featured), has been chosen to complement the gospel passage, by either anticipating the message of Jesus or revealing some truth about him (sometimes related as biblical prophecy to its fulfillment in Christ) or otherwise presenting similar themes to those found in the gospel.

The second reading is generally from one of the Letters of Paul or one of the other apostolic authors (James, Jude, Peter, John), and is usually read for a number of Sundays in a row (depending on the length of the letter).

Given the above configuration of scriptural readings, my reflection for each Sunday generally centres on the gospel reading, with references of shorter or longer length on the first reading and, usually, a brief allusion to the second reading. On occasion, because of the importance of the text or to offer a variety in the focus of the homily, my focus falls on the second reading or, less frequently still, on the psalm.

II. Luke's Theological and Spiritual Emphases

In reflecting on Luke's account of Jesus' career during Year C, Christians will come to know the emphases Luke has made his own in presenting the Good News.

More than other evangelists, Luke stresses the "world-affirming" dimension of Jesus' ministry; he locates Jesus not only within the salvation history of God's chosen people but within the history of the whole human race. Thus, Luke refers both to the leaders of Israel and to figures like the Caesars (Augustus and Tiberius) who played key roles on the world stage, where Jesus of Nazareth belongs.

Luke's Gospel highlights God's designs as the reversal of human values and expectations.

God demonstrated a preferential love for the poor, the afflicted and the outcast as the starting point for summoning all humanity to salvation.

Luke underlines the importance of faith and of prayer, giving prominence to the Holy Spirit's role in the life of Jesus and his disciples. The theme of Jesus at prayer will recur in this commentary and is mentioned below regarding Jesus' prayer on the Mount of Olives and on the Cross.

[For those wishing to explore prayer in their own lives in tandem with reading this volume, the last section of the *Catechism of the Catholic Church*, on Prayer (Rome, 1992, #2558–2865) is a rich resource. So, too, is Pope Benedict's Post-Synodal Apostolic Exhortation *Verbum Domini*, where he particularly recommends the practice of *Lectio divina* (a "holy reading") of biblical texts (Rome: September 30, 2010, #87). This method is illustrated in my presentation of the readings on the

First Sunday of Lent and may be adapted to the scriptural texts of other Sundays.]

Luke shows that conversion implies a change in one's behaviour, and he accentuates the presence and contribution of women among Jesus' disciples.

Above all, Luke emphasizes the orderly transition from the ministry of Jesus to the mission of the Twelve Apostles. The evangelist shows that God blessed the transition from early Church patterns in the apostolic era to later structures governed by elders appointed in apostolic succession.

Though many of the early Church's struggles might appear to have been chaotic, the development of the Church came about following a divinely ordained plan so that people's faith might be firmly grounded (Luke 1.1-4).

During this liturgical year, we will see how Luke explores dimensions in the disciples' experiences with Jesus that get below surface appearances. One example is Peter's sense of unworthiness at his call (Luke 5.1-11). Another is a forgiven woman's love overflowing into tears that bathed the feet of Jesus (7.36-50). Others still are a cleansed leper's joy that had to say "thank you" (17.11-19), and the recollection by the Emmaus disciples that their hearts burned within them as Jesus opened the meaning of the Scriptures to them (24.13-35).

These themes and others are found in parables and narratives unique to the Third Gospel.

Once one has detected the outline in the gospel, we see how it is fleshed out in the life of the Church and are invited to see it in our own Church's life (in Canada, in this diocese, in this parish; within our world of relativism and of aggressive secularism, of globalization and instantaneous media, of creativity, scientific breakthroughs, of energy and heightened consciousness regarding the environment, and so on).

III. Luke's Travel Narrative

A feature of Luke's Gospel that distinguishes it from others is the "Travel Narrative" (9.51–19.27). This unit begins dramatically with the notice that "When the days drew near for him to be taken up, Jesus set his face to go to Jerusalem".

The material found in the Travel Narrative consists mainly of sayings of Jesus paralleled in Matthew's Gospel (some scholars attribute this collection of Jesus' teaching to a hypothetical source designated "Q" – shorthand for *Quelle*, the German word meaning "source"). Whether this is the case or not does not affect our interpretation; what is important when comparing the texts common to Matthew and Luke is probing the patterns that regularly distinguish each evangelist's tendencies or emphases.

As well, we find in the travel account traditions unique to Luke's Gospel (such as the parables of the Good Samaritan; the Prodigal Son; the Rich Man and Lazarus; the Dishonest Steward; the Pharisee and the Tax-collector; as well as stories of Jesus' encounter with people such as Martha and Mary or Zacchaeus).

Only towards the end of Jesus' journey did Luke refer to traditions he held in common with Mark (cf. Luke 18.15-43; Mark 10.13-52). While it is hard to pinpoint one predominant reason that led Luke to structure a large block of the gospel tradition in this way, scholars note that Luke's account of Paul's ministry in Acts parallels Jesus' last days by being described as a voyage from Jerusalem to Rome. Several times in Acts, the Christian movement is called "the Way" (9.2). This suggests that following Jesus consists not in staying put, but in committing oneself to serve within a dynamic movement.

Even though this collection known as the Travel Narrative is eclectic, underneath its surface simplicity it packs power to engage, instruct and even unsettle disciples.

The beginning of Jesus' ministry reached a climax with rejection by his townspeople (Luke 4.28-30). So the start of Jesus' great journey is also marked by the Samaritans' rejection of him (because his face was set towards Jerusalem).

Later, Jesus' ministry in Jerusalem would culminate in the ultimate rejection when he was handed over to crucifixion and death. Paradoxically, all these rejections led the Good News to be offered to more and more people who were reckoned initially as far from God's saving purpose.

IV. Luke's Passion and Resurrection Narrative

Each evangelist, while making use of ancient Christian traditions concerning the last hours of Jesus, quotes the Scriptures to give to these moments his own reflections on these pivotal moments of salvation history.

For example, Mark gives a stark picture of the brokenness Jesus suffered on the Cross ("My God, my God, why have you forsaken me?" [15.34]), while Matthew, as he did with Jesus' infancy, shows how all that happened was "so that the scriptures of the prophets may be fulfilled" (26.56). John shows that, for the eyes of faith, and despite appearances to the contrary, Jesus was in charge of all that transpired in the Passion, which was the supreme moment of his glorification: "when Jesus knew that all was now finished, he said (in order to fulfill the scripture), 'I am thirsty'" (19.28).

Luke's account of the closing days of Jesus' ministry and his Passion narrative draw out emphases given by him to the Lord's life earlier on. During the messianic act of entering Jerusalem, Luke shows that this was not an act of political messianism. Rather, he notes that those who acclaimed Jesus were not the citizens of Jerusalem but "the whole multitude of the disciples" (19.37). Their acclamations sought to praise God "for all the deeds of power that they had seen" (19.37) in the healings that characterized Jesus' ministry. This is not simply the glorification of Jesus, but praise of God for Jesus.

In the Passion, Luke takes pains to show that the Roman authorities have no cause to fear the followers of Jesus. The accusation against Jesus, that he was "perverting our nation, forbidding us to pay taxes to the emperor, and saying that he himself is the Messiah, a king" (23.2) is judged unfounded by Pilate ("I have examined him in your presence and have not found this man guilty of any of your charges against him" [23.14]). To underline this point, at Jesus' death, the centurion declares, "Certainly this man was innocent" (23.47).

Just as Luke depicted Jesus at prayer at all the high points of his ministry (the night before the choice of the Twelve, at the Transfiguration, prior to Peter's confession), so, too, does he depict Jesus praying during the Passion. Jesus reassured Peter, when foretelling his coming denials, that "I have prayed for you that your own faith may not fail" (22.32).

The prayer of Jesus on the Mount of Olives becomes an agony that leads him to pray more intensively, "Father, if you are willing, remove this cup from me; yet not my will but yours be done" (22.42).

With the comforting brought by the angel, Jesus regains his serenity and invokes the Father's pardon of those who crucify him ("Father, forgive them, for they do not know what they are doing" [23.34]). Likewise, on the Cross, Jesus' final prayer is one of confidently entrusting himself to God: "Father, into your hands I commend my spirit" (23.46), with words that echo those of the psalmist (Psalm 31.5).

Luke's theological view of Jesus is that he is God's messiah, God's Son carried up into the new world with God in heaven (beginning at 9.51). And from the new world of his Ascension and with God, Jesus now guides the Church he left his apostles and their successors to manage until he comes again in glory. Each year is an opportunity to discover it fresh, anew. Let us rejoice that in Year C we will do so guided by Luke, the evangelist of God's mercy to the poor and needy, including ourselves.

V. Preparing for Sunday Mass

Each homilist, study group or other interpreter of the Sunday Scriptures (such as those engaged in children's Liturgy of the Word) will devise their own appropriate manner of using this book. The following thoughts may help those looking for a methodology.

The most important starting point is to read through the gospel of a particular Sunday or solemnity and then the first reading several times, looking for common and differing emphases as well as any structural features that stand out.

A second point would be to list problem areas in interpretation. In the texts, which matters or issues might contemporary readers not understand? Which issues might they struggle with?

At this time, one could read the reflections on the readings to see what clarifications are offered. As each text is very brief (somewhere around 700 words), it is not likely that every difficulty a reader might have will be resolved. Here we see the importance of having access to a biblical commentary or biblical dictionary. I have often found that commentators touch on every issue except the one that interests me; hence the need for several other tools.

Biblical scholars should not have the only word or the last word in interpreting texts for the Church. Sometimes others outside the guild have something to offer. For example, David Lyle Jeffrey's recent commentary on Luke in the *Brazos Theological Commentary on the Bible* invites non-Biblicist academics to interpret a text (Grand Rapids: Baker Publishing, 2012). Novelists, too, have insights to share on the world and Christian imagination regarding Luke; two of these that come to mind are Taylor Caldwell's epic, *Dear and Glorious Physician* (original 1958; reprint San Francisco: Ignatius, 2008) and the more recent novel *Theophilos* by the Canadian writer Michael O'Brien (San Francisco: Ignatius, 2010).

Next, the second reading could be read meditatively, with the same pattern used in contemplating the gospel and first reading. Because all the texts for solemnities, Advent and Lent are chosen in function of the feast or liturgical season, the second reading on those occasions will more generally fit with the gospel and first reading. On the Sundays of Ordinary Time or in the Easter season, meanwhile, the second readings are continuous.

Finally, the psalm could be prayed as a closing devotional exercise that picks up a theme of the Sunday or feast day.

May Mary, Mother of the Word Incarnate, who remains for the Church the model for believers who strive to "hear the word of God and obey it" (Luke 11.28), intercede for all who will use this book to deepen their knowledge of God's self-communication in his holy word.

First Sunday of Advent

"To Stand Before the Son of Man"

* Jeremiah 33.14-16
* Psalm 25
* 1 Thessalonians 3.12–4.2
* Luke 21.25-28, 34-36

As this Sunday marks the beginning of a new liturgical season (Year "C"), the gospel readings are now taken principally from St. Luke. The first Sunday of Advent takes up where the previous Church year ended, with a focus on the Parousia (the "advent" or "coming") of Jesus, the Son of Man, in glory. This Lord will come at the end of time to usher in the fullness of God's kingdom.

The field of biblical and Church teaching about the last things is known as "eschatology". In addition to matters associated with Jesus' second coming, eschatological truths deal with the realities implied by death, judgment, heaven and hell. These subjects are not simply arcane topics of interest only to specialists. They are important aspects of the Christian faith that have a bearing on how disciples live their lives in the world.

Whereas the other two synoptic evangelists presented the teaching of Jesus about the end of the world in one large block (Mark 13.1-37; Matthew 24.1–25.46), Luke included several extended blocks of eschatological teaching by Jesus (12.13-59; 17.20-37; 19.11-28; and 21.7-38). It is as if Luke wished to make the point that there is a dimension of end-time thinking that needs to be woven into the fabric of each Christian's life.

As they read Luke's two-volume work (the Gospel and the Acts of the Apostles) late in the first century, Christians would have been aware that Jesus also had accurately predicted the fall of Jerusalem and the destruction of the Temple in 70 AD (Luke 21.8-11, 20-24). Accordingly, they would have had confidence in Jesus' predictions about happenings still to come, the theme of today's gospel. Jesus' words about the end speak of the cosmic portents that will take place and of the reactions then of people who do not understand what these happenings mean ("people will faint from fear and foreboding of what is coming upon the world").

Awareness that Jesus could come at any time (at the Parousia or in one's personal death) should be part of each disciple's outlook on life. He or she would then realize that there is no need to fear encountering the glorified Christ, when "they will see 'the Son of Man coming in a cloud' with power and great glory".

The Lord Jesus, the one who is coming – the righteous branch that God caused to spring from David's line, as Jeremiah prophesied – is well known to Christian disciples from their prayer and their encounters with him in the sacraments. The confidence the Christian should possess then will allow him or her to "stand up and raise your heads, because your redemption is drawing near".

Luke alone recounted the cure by Jesus of a woman who "was bent over and was quite unable to stand up straight" because she had been bound by Satan for eighteen years (13.11-17). Her healing was a sign of the liberation God offers to all, something that will be fully realized only in that final redemption to be unveiled at the end of the days of this world. Each believer's confidence that this promise will come true for them at Jesus' coming should prompt them to lift their heads high, "to stand before the Son of Man" confidently on that day.

Jesus' message ended with a moral exhortation that his disciples' acceptance of the truths laid out have a bearing on their lives. Above all, they must keep themselves at the ready, praying and being "alert at all times".

In other places, Jesus described his coming as being sudden – like labour pains that come upon a woman – or unexpected, like the coming of a thief in the night. In Luke's account of the apocalyptic address, Jesus also used the springing of a snare "trap" to describe how the Great Day of the Lord would come upon people unawares.

The universality of the coming day of judgment is underlined by Jesus: "it will come upon all who live on the face of the whole earth". Jesus' listeners should beware of letting their way of life become burdened or dulled by "dissipation and drunkenness and the worries of this life" – by excessive solicitude for material things.

In the second reading, Paul informs the Thessalonians that, ultimately, it is God's work in Christian lives that makes it possible for them to grow in love, to be strengthened in holiness and to be blameless before God when Jesus comes. God, then, is the ground of Christian hope in the future.

Second Sunday of Advent

A Wilderness in One's Heart

* Baruch 5.1-9
* Psalm 126
* Philippians 1.3-6, 8-11
* Luke 3.1-6

In the annual observance of Advent, the four Sundays feature the various "comings" of Jesus. On the first Sunday, the emphasis lies on Christian yearning for the return of the Lord Jesus in glory at the end of time. On the middle two Sundays, Christians turn their attention to the preaching of John the Baptist, when Jesus was about to inaugurate his ministry. Finally, on the fourth Sunday, Christians ready themselves to recall Christ's coming in the human condition at his birth by focusing on the dispositions of his mother, Mary.

Advent virtues, then, run the gamut of fervent hope to humble receptivity. This Sunday and next, the appropriate Christian disposition is repentance – with openness to being purified. Such a spirit of repentance – and the joy that comes in its wake – colours the whole of the prophecy of Baruch, from which today's first reading is taken.

Baruch was the confidante, secretary and disciple of the prophet Jeremiah (Jeremiah 32.12). In the late sixth century BC, he was taken with Jeremiah to exile in Egypt (43.6). One tradition says he died there, while another says he was carried off later and died in Babylon. Because of his great stature, the result of his association with Jeremiah, various writings were attributed to him.

The Book of Baruch is not found in the Hebrew Bible. Though not considered a canonical writing by Protestants and Jews, Catholics regard it as a "deuterocanonical" work – in other words, accepted as part of the official canon of Scripture. Probably it was written around 100 BC to express a spirituality of exile – as the Jews had experienced it in Babylon – along with fervent devotion for Torah and a spirit of penance for sin.

Baruch maintains that, once God's people turn from disobedience, they can hear again God's messianic promises and summons to rejoice. "Take off your garment of your sorrow and affliction ... [and] put on the robe of the righteousness that comes from God". Jerusalem is charged to stand and look towards the east to see the exiles returning "at the word of the Holy One, rejoicing that God has remembered them".

The wilderness east of Jerusalem – hinted at by Baruch – is the scene of John the Baptist's preaching. Baruch's motif, "God has ordered that every high mountain and the everlasting hills be made low and the valleys filled up, to make level ground", recalls the promises of God proclaimed by Second Isaiah (40.3-5). Luke evokes Isaiah in his account of John the Baptist's preaching. Indeed, the Baptist's citation of Isaiah extends to the entire world the blessing that Baruch had promised the returning Jewish exiles: "all flesh shall see the salvation of God".

In salvation history, the wilderness or desert held a painful yet privileged position. It recalled Israel's period of testing and rebellion, which had also proven to be a place of grace and revelation. To go into the wilderness, then, meant facing one's fragility, one's weakness and sin and, in doing so, experiencing the corresponding possibility of repentance and renewal.

Life in the wilderness forces a person to focus on the basics: the need for water and shelter against the heat. Solidarity with fellow pilgrims on the journey and hospitality to strangers become core values. The trials associated with survival bring out the best and the worst in people. The unremitting demands of desert life uncover the hardness of one's heart, as well as the potential to be broken open and to encounter God. Such was the experience of the patriarchs and of the Israelites who took part in the Exodus. John the Baptist wanted to open his hearers to such realities when he preached "a baptism of repentance for the forgiveness of sins". The Advent liturgy challenges today's disciples of Jesus to such graced moments now.

In Baruch, the exile was transformed from an exterior chastisement in history into an inner experience whose spiritual depths opened God's people to repentance, to love of divine wisdom in the Law and to the joys of the coming days of messianic fulfillment.

Advent invites Christians to make the wilderness an interior experience that touches their hearts, leading them to discover God's call to repentance, to a renewed offer of forgiveness and to new life. Among the ways Catholics can celebrate this inward experience is the Advent celebration of the sacrament of reconciliation.

Third Sunday of Advent

The Joy of a Changed Outlook

* Zephaniah 3.14-18
* Isaiah 12.2-6
* Philippians 4.4-7
* Luke 3.10-18

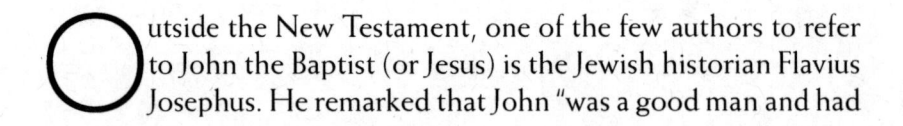

Outside the New Testament, one of the few authors to refer to John the Baptist (or Jesus) is the Jewish historian Flavius Josephus. He remarked that John "was a good man and had exhorted the Jews to lead virtuous lives, to practice justice towards their fellows and piety towards God and, so doing, to join in baptism" (*Jewish Antiquities*, 18.116). Josephus went on to note that righteous behaviour was necessary for people's baptism to be acceptable to God. In other words, heeding the call to conversion implies a change in one's lifestyle.

The New Testament stresses the close connection between the teaching of John the Baptist and Jesus, a point Josephus does not make. Today's gospel shows John calling the crowds, tax collectors and soldiers to a new way of relating to others. Like Jesus, John preached repentance ("a change of mind, a change of heart") to those who came to him at the banks of the Jordan. Each group wanted to know what practical bearing such a change of disposition might have on their lives ("What should we do?"). In reply, the Baptist gave a (non-exhaustive) set of examples of what such new thinking might look like in daily life.

John summoned the crowds who enjoyed the blessing of material goods to share them with the destitute poor ("Whoever has two coats must share with anyone who has none; and whoever has food must do likewise"). He invited the tax collectors, detested as the instrument of the Roman occupying power and presumed by their fellow Jews to be extortionist, to live in social justice with their compatriots, avoiding the corruption that typified their profession ("Collect no more than the amount prescribed for you").

Then John addressed the soldiers, men serving in the army of Herod Antipas as police, who supported the tax collectors in levying tolls and duties, urging them not to shake people down. Poorly paid, soldiers were tempted to use their position to extort money from people by intimidation or trumped-up charges. Instead, Jesus' forerunner exhorted them to be sons of Abraham by keeping the seventh and eighth commandments ("Do not extort money from anyone by threats or false accusation"). The Baptist's last words to the soldiers ("be satisfied with your wages") may also be an allusion to the tenth commandment, not to covet what belongs to others.

John the Baptist showed himself as personally selfless when he testified to Jesus ("one who is more powerful than I is coming"). He also showed humility in heralding the one who would baptize God's people with the Holy Spirit and fire ("I am not worthy to untie the thong of his sandals"). John concluded his preaching by observing that the coming Day of Judgment would reveal the truth about how people have lived, as wheat and chaff are separated at harvest-time.

Luke closed his account of John the Baptist's witness to Jesus with the remark "So, with many other exhortations, John proclaimed good news to the people". The third evangelist knew from his own experience that the change in life that allowed one to live according to God's purposes was, despite its cost, "good news" and the source of great joy. Not surprisingly, then, Luke – more than the other evangelists – emphasized the joy that comes to those who live by the message common to Jesus and to John, his herald.

The joy of the transforming power of the gospel serves as the theme of today's entire "Gaudete" ("Rejoicing") Sunday liturgy. In writing to the Philippian Christians, Paul challenged them to a continuously joyful outlook ("Rejoice in the Lord always; again I will say, Rejoice"). They had been remarkable for their spirit of self-sacrificing love towards Paul, supporting him financially at a time when no other Church had done so. They had every reason to be joyful.

The seventh-century BC prophet Zephaniah spoke of God's judgment on Jerusalem and Judea. This would be a prelude to their conversion and transformation into a poor and humble people in whose presence the righteous God could live ("The Lord, your God, is in your midst ... he will renew you in his love").

Fourth Sunday of Advent

Bethlehem's Lowliness and Mary's Humility

* Micah 5.2-5a
* Psalm 80
* Hebrews 10.5-10
* Luke 1.39-45

The prophet Micah lived in the eighth and seventh centuries BC. Micah's powerful utterances are credited with converting King Hezekiah, who ruled from 715 to 686 BC. This led to the reform of the southern kingdom of Judah and the renewal of its worship and life.

False prophets in Micah's day ingratiated themselves with the rich. Micah, zealous for justice, preached God's judgment on sinfulness as well as God's favour towards all who repented of injustice. Micah briefly summarized God's expectations of human behaviour as follows: "what does the Lord require of you but to do justice, and to love kindness, and to walk humbly with your God?" (6.8).

The book of Micah has been compared to a preacher's file of sermons – oracles of doom mingled with words of encouragement. Scholarly effort seeks to define how the book's chapters fit together. In one scheme, the middle section (chapters 3 to 5) is entitled "false leaders denounced, a righteous king promised".

Today's first reading, then, contrasts Israelite kings of the past with the glorious leader God has in mind, "whose origin is from of old, from ancient days". Since kings born in Jerusalem had failed to meet the ideals proposed for them, God promised to go back to Bethlehem – to the birthplace of King David – to find a messiah worthy of his lineage.

Micah's stress on the names Ephrathah, Bethlehem and Judea emphasized David's pristine origins as Jesse's son rather than the later, decadent phase of his life in Jerusalem. As the youngest, David was insignificant by comparison with his brothers. Still, God chose him to rule over Israel, making a new beginning for the kingship after Saul's failures.

Though Bethlehem remained "one of the little clans of Judea", God's intent was once again to bring forth from its midst "one who is to rule in Israel". God's choice of Bethlehem meant that, paradoxically, the most insignificant of places would bring forth the most distinguished leader.

Micah concluded his prophecy of God's purpose by revealing that the coming shepherd-king would extend God's rule to the ends of the earth. With such a leader, it would be possible for God's people and the whole world to dwell in security and peace ("he shall stand and feed his flock in the strength of the Lord ... and he shall be peace").

When the New Testament comes to describe the way in which God fulfilled the ancient promises concerning his messiah, the words "lowliness", "humility" and "hiddenness" are apt modifiers. In the last days of the reign of Herod the Great, who died in 4 BC, God sent angelic messages to an otherwise inconsequential couple, Mary and Joseph, announcing the virginal conception of Jesus. They lived in the Galilean backwater of Nazareth, a town even more insignificant than Bethlehem. In fear and trembling – but with faith as well – they agreed to participate in God's design for humanity's salvation.

In Luke's Gospel, the angel Gabriel announced to Mary that she would conceive, by the overshadowing of the Holy Spirit, a son who would inherit forever the throne of his ancestor David. To illustrate that "nothing will be impossible with God", Gabriel pointed to the conception of a child by Mary's kinswoman, Elizabeth, despite her old age. This was the prelude to today's gospel of the Visitation, in which Mary, "with haste", made the approximately four-day, 130-kilometre journey from Nazareth to "a Judean town in the hill country" to visit her relative.

No motive is given, but the fact that Mary stayed with Elizabeth until the time of her cousin's delivery suggests service and support. This is the selflessness Mary's son Jesus would later teach and that Hebrews, in today's second reading, attributes to him: "See, God, I have come to do your will".

In humility, Mary declared her praise of God in the Magnificat, which follows Elizabeth's greetings in today's gospel. Christians have made Elizabeth's praise of Mary their own through the ages: "Blessed are you among women, and blessed is the fruit of your womb". Mary is blessed, above all, for her humble faith, which is a model for all believers. "Blessed is she who believed that there would be a fulfillment of what was spoken to her by the Lord"!

The Holy Family of Jesus, Mary and Joseph

Anxiety and Dialogue in the Holy Family

* 1 Samuel 1.20-22, 24-28
* Psalm 84
* 1 John 3.1-2, 21-24
* Luke 2.41-52

A couple who are friends of mine were speaking recently of their children, and specifically of the challenge to listen attentively as each child shares with one or both of them their experiences, questions, doubts, fears, dreams and accomplishments. Since they have a large family, this can prove quite demanding. It is a set of conversations that seemingly need never end, even when the children become adults.

We see a reflection of this family need to dialogue continually through a gospel episode lived out by the Holy Family in the Joyful Mystery of Jesus' being lost and found during a Passover pilgrimage to Jerusalem.

When, after three days of searching, Mary and Joseph found the Child Jesus in the Temple, "sitting among the teachers, listening to them and asking them questions", they revealed to him their astonishment and the worry that had preoccupied them: "Why have you treated us like this? Look, your father and I have been searching for you in great anxiety".

His answer, "Did you not know that I must be in my Father's house?" (or "about my Father's business") left them perplexed ("But they did not understand what he said to them"). The experience would have to be incorporated into their ongoing discovery of who this Holy Child truly was as God's Son ("his mother treasured all these things in her heart").

Mary's reply at the Annunciation – "Here am I, the servant of the Lord: let it be with me according to your word" – had made obedience to God's will her priority in life. Even so, she would not escape having to struggle to sort out the events God's providence would bring into her life and that of her remarkable Son. Including the implications of the fact that he "went down with them and came to Nazareth, and was obedient to them ... and [that] Jesus increased in wisdom and in years, and in favour with God and human beings".

It is a rare family even today that cannot identify with the confusion and shock of Jesus' parents at his words, which placed a deep gap between the devotion he owed them in filial piety and the powerful attraction he felt towards a higher vocation.

God began to prepare a whole new order in divine–human relationships by the Incarnation. The new values, however, began unremarkably in the simple piety of Jewish parents who communicated their religious values by making the long and arduous pilgrimage every year to Jerusalem for Passover.

An earlier religious renewal took place in Israel's history with the birth of another special child, the prophet Samuel. The early stories of Samuel's birth and childhood contrast the decaying priesthood represented by Eli and his sons with the prophet's dynamic new leadership (1 Samuel 1–3).

Shiloh was a major sanctuary of the Israelite tribes and the resting place for the Ark of God. The annual visit there was a time when Hannah's childlessness became a burden to her. In distress, she made a prayer and took a vow, asking God to remember her.

As her song of jubilation – close in spirit to Mary's Magnificat – later makes clear, Hannah assumed God cares for those without status (1 Samuel 2.1-11). She straightforwardly asked God for a male child. And pledged to give back the gift she would receive, dedicating him as a Nazirite, consecrated individuals who show dedication to God by abstaining from strong drink and never cutting their hair.

God "remembered" Hannah, so she conceived and gave birth to a son. Samuel was not immediately dedicated to God's service; rather, Hannah waited until he was weaned, then brought him to Shiloh with appropriate offerings and sacrifices. Hannah declared that her child Samuel was God's response to "the petition that I made to him". "Samuel" thereby gets associated with the Hebrew verb *sa'al*, which can mean "to ask" or "to lend" ("Therefore I have lent him to the Lord; as long as he lives, he is given to the Lord").

In the second reading, St. John says that Christians are already by adoption what Jesus was by nature: God's children ("we are God's children now"). Jesus' disciples believe that their future at the end of time will be glorious ("when he is revealed, we will be like him, for we will see him as he is").

Epiphany of the Lord

"We Observed His Star at Its Rising"

* Isaiah 60.1-6
* Psalm 72
* Ephesians 3.2-3a, 5-6
* Matthew 2.1-12

Each Christmas season, radio and television broadcasts feature scholars casting seasonal skepticism on the gospel accounts of the birth of Jesus. These pronouncements can be quite unsettling for Christians who cherish the narratives of the birth of Jesus and see in them rich images of God and our Lord that speak powerfully to their lives of faith.

Still, every year around Christmas, newspapers also feature stories about astronomers describing a conjunction of planets or stars that may fulfill the description given in Matthew's account of the Magi following a star to the newborn Christ child.

Thus, scientists note there was a coming together of the planets Jupiter and Venus in 7 BC. Shortly afterwards, there was the extremely rare – every 794 years – conjunction of Jupiter, Saturn and the Sign of the Fishes.

If Jupiter was the star of the universe, Saturn the planet of Palestine, and the constellation of the Fishes the sign of the last days, someone could deduce from the rare heavenly movements that the ruler of the end times would soon appear in the land of Israel.

The accounts found in Matthew and Luke differ considerably from each other. Only Luke tells about the census, the heavenly host of angels and the shepherds. Matthew alone notes the appearance of the Magi, the gifts of gold, frankincense and myrrh, the flight into Egypt and the slaughter of the Holy Innocents.

We cannot deduce from the gospel story that the Magi arrived on camels. Rather, this idea may derive from today's responsorial Psalm 72 or from the passage read from Isaiah, both of which have been associated with the Epiphany's solemnity. Nor do we know that there were three Magi (this is deduced from the gifts mentioned) or what their names were (Caspar, Balthasar and Melchior are late additions to the Epiphany tradition).

Despite their differences, the evangelists Matthew and Luke agree on several points: that Jesus was virginally conceived; that he was born in Bethlehem in Judea in the days of King Herod; and that his parents were named Mary and Joseph.

Since Herod the Great died in 4 BC, Jesus must have been born between 7 and 4 BC (blame for the incorrect division between BC and AD is laid at the feet of the medieval monk Denis, who erred in his calculations).

Herod was part Jewish and part Idumean. Although a skilled builder of monumental buildings such as the Jerusalem Temple, Herod's blood connection with Edom, biblical Israel's sworn enemy, made him detestable to religiously observant Jews.

Paranoia characterized Herod in his latter years. Thus he murdered his wife Mariamne, her mother, two of her sons, and even his eldest son. His furtive dealings with the Magi ("Herod secretly called for the wise men"), his cowardly lies ("bring me word so that I may also go and pay him homage") and, later, his ruthless slaughter of innocent boys two years and younger show the illegitimacy of his claim to the kingship when contrasted with the divinely sanctioned newborn "Messiah".

From their reading of the Scriptures, "the scribes of the people" assisted the Magi, whose astrological calculations could not bring them fully to Jesus. For such instruction about God's promises is one function of God's word.

The Scriptures, specifically the prophet Micah, pointed the Magi towards Bethlehem. When once again the star appeared – for revelation and nature together lead to understanding of divine mysteries – the Magi were filled with that joy that God alone can give. They delighted when the star stopped over the house where Jesus stayed.

In surrendering precious gifts, the Magi offered worship to the new king ("On entering the house, they saw the child with Mary his Mother; and they knelt down and paid him homage"). The Magi may be understood as prototypes of all Jesus' future disciples, who gladly give up earthly treasures for heavenly treasures (cf. Matthew 6.19-21; 19.21).

Epiphany means "manifestation" and tells of the Gentiles coming to know God's Son as their Saviour. In the words of the letter to the Ephesians, concerning Jesus' death and resurrection, thereby "the Gentiles have become fellow heirs [with believing Jews], members of the same body [the Church, Christ's Body], and sharers in the promise in Christ Jesus through the Gospel".

The Baptism of the Lord

"Jesus Also Had Been Baptized and Was Praying"

* Isaiah 40.1-5, 9-11
* Psalm 104
* Titus 2.11-14; 3.4-7
* Luke 3.15-16, 21-22

After detailing at some length John's preaching ministry, which culminated in the Baptist's imprisonment by Herod Antipas (3.1-20), Luke offered his readers a terse description of Jesus' baptism (3.21-22).

The son of Herod the Great, Antipas ruled Galilee and Perea from 4 BC to 39 AD. John the Baptist had rebuked Herod publicly for his unlawful marriage to Herodias and "because of all the evil things that Herod had done". Herod's worst crime was to silence the criticism of his morals by locking John up in the hilltop fortress of Machaerus, where later he would meet a martyr's death.

By contrast with the ruler who shirked responsibility for his immorality, Jesus – one who was innocent and without sin – stood in solidarity with sinful humanity, coming to be baptized with repentant Israelites ("all the people were baptized"). Jesus underwent John's water baptism, which imaged and pointed towards that greater baptism in the Holy Spirit, which he would confer after his death and resurrection.

Only the evangelist Luke notes that Jesus was at prayer at the time of his baptism. This observation is part of a Lukan pattern, which depicts Jesus praying on numerous occasions: such as on the night before he chose his twelve apostles and delivered the great inaugural sermon (6.12); prior to eliciting Peter's confession that he was the "Messiah of God" (9.18); at the Transfiguration (9.29); and as a prelude to instructing his disciples to pray the "Lord's Prayer" and to trust in God's eagerness to give them the Holy Spirit (11.1-13).

Luke says that Jesus told his disciples a parable about a widow who insistently sought and obtained justice from an unjust judge in order to illustrate "their need to pray always and not to lose heart" (18.1-8).

While prayer is especially fitting in moments of crisis (for example, on the Mount of Olives, Jesus "prayed more earnestly, and his sweat became like great drops of blood falling down on the ground" [22.44]), it ought, as well, to characterize the daily routine of disciples as it did the life of their Master.

Luke's description of Jesus' baptism showed his devotion and nearness to God – that he looked to God at every stage of his mission. This impression is heightened by two elements: the physical sign of the Spirit descending upon Jesus and the endorsement of Jesus through God's voice from heaven: "This is my Son, the Beloved, with whom I am well pleased".

The voice from heaven addressed Jesus in terms that echo biblical texts, though which ones precisely is debated by scholars. Good cases can be made that Psalm 2.7 (a royal psalm that would identify Jesus as God's Son with regal powers) and Isaiah 42.1 (a text that would proclaim Jesus as God's humble, Spirit-led servant) underlie the gospel's formulation of God's approval of Jesus.

But the experience of Jesus' baptism was not only his. For with the opening of the heavens came the Spirit's descent. The visible nature of this occurrence is manifest in the description of the Spirit's alighting on Jesus "descending like a dove". Two passages from Genesis (God's brooding over the waters at creation [1.2] and Noah's dove [8.8-12], symbolizing the end of judgment and the beginning of grace) suggest that what happened in Jesus' baptism inaugurated a new era in divine–human relations.

Second Isaiah's proclamation of the dawning of a new era began with words of consolation: "Comfort, O comfort my people". For Israel's sins had been atoned ("her penalty is paid ... she has received from the Lord's hand double for all her sins"), a reality Christians believe has been definitively achieved in the obedient disposition of Jesus' identification with sinners.

In other words, what Jesus accomplished on the Cross began at his baptism. The time of Israel's dispersal is also ended; the time for unity has come ("[the Lord God] will feed his flock like a shepherd").

The epistle to Titus comments on the new beginning for humanity that started in Jesus' baptism and extends to more and more people through Christian baptism: "When the goodness and loving kindness of God our Saviour appeared, he saved us, not because of any works of righteousness that we had done, but according to his mercy, through the water of rebirth and renewal by the Holy Spirit".

Second Sunday in Ordinary Time

Jesus' Presence Blesses a Wedding

* Isaiah 62.1-5
* Psalm 96
* 1 Corinthians 12.4-11
* John 2.1-12

In Catholic teaching, "the matrimonial covenant, by which a man and a woman establish between themselves a partnership of the whole of life, is by its nature ordered towards the good of the spouses and the procreation and education of offspring; this covenant between baptized persons has been raised by Christ the Lord to the dignity of a sacrament" (*Code of Canon Law*, 1055).

Spouses freely entering a marriage make an indissoluble commitment of fidelity to each other until death. Unless dispensed for good reason (as when a Catholic marries someone from another Christian tradition or another faith), Catholics marry before two witnesses in a church ceremony presided over by a priest or deacon.

The liturgies of both Latin and Eastern Church traditions abound in prayers invoking God's grace and blessing for couples entering upon a lifelong project. In the solemn invocation (*epiclesis*) in the rites of matrimony, "the spouses receive the Holy Spirit as the communion of love of Christ and the Church" (*Catechism of the Catholic Church*, #1624).

Understanding the solemn and sacramental nature of marriage, the Church has noted with joy that, on the threshold of his public ministry, Jesus performed his first "sign", at his mother's request, during a wedding feast.

With notes of joy and abundance, this wedding feast miracle inaugurates Jesus' ministry, a function that Jesus' inaugural sermon at Nazareth fulfilled in Luke's Gospel, as we shall see next week.

The Fourth Evangelist affords the reader only scant details of the miracle of water changed into wine: when ("on the third day" – a veiled reference to resurrection faith?); who ("the mother of Jesus" – she is never called Mary in John's Gospel; Jesus; the disciples; servants); and where ("Cana of Galilee" – a place unattested in gospel traditions but that features in another miracle in the Johannine tradition [cf. 4.46-54]).

A simple problem establishes the occasion for Jesus' intervention: the wine has run out. This is communicated to Jesus by his mother. Though she asked for nothing directly, Mary presumed her Son would attend to the situation.

Though Jesus' address to his mother ("Woman") strikes the modern ear as harsh or rude, it is neither. Jesus addressed the Canaanite woman this way (Matthew 15.28) and, later in the gospel, he used the same form to address his mother under the Cross (John 19.26) and to greet Mary Magdalene on Easter morning (20.15).

The formulaic address and Jesus' other words to his mother ("what concern is that to you and to me?") established distance and played down family ties in order to highlight, instead, dimensions of faith.

While the term "hour" can refer to passing time (cf. John 1.39), generally in John's Gospel it points to the moment of Jesus' "glorification", comprised of his Passion, death, resurrection and Ascension (cf. 7.30; 8.20; 12.23; 13.1; 17.1). On Jesus' lips, "hour" can also refer to the moment of God's eschatological fulfillment (4.21; 5.28).

Jesus twice paradoxically declared that the future reality had already become present in his presence and words: "the hour is coming, and is now here, when the true worshippers will worship the Father in spirit and truth" (John 4.23; cf. 5.25).

The coming "hour" demands faith, and it is this believing stance that Jesus' mother anticipated when she said to the servants, "Do whatever he tells you". Though his "hour" would not come fully until his being lifted up on the Cross, the faith of the mother of Jesus anticipated the fruits of his glorification ("Jesus did this, the first of his signs, in Cana of Galilee, and revealed his glory").

The abundance of "the good wine" brought joy and honour to a couple on the verge of tears and disgrace. More appropriately, however, this first of Jesus' signs evoked faith among his first followers ("and his disciples believed in him").

Third Isaiah used a joyous wedding feast to announce removal of Israel's shame experienced by exile from the land of Israel. God's love for his people was expressed in nuptial imagery, "as the bridegroom rejoices over the bride, so shall your God rejoice over you".

God's ongoing delight in the Church appears in the spiritual gifts abundantly at work within the Church – whether married, celibate or single: "there are varieties of activities, but it is the same God who activates all of them in everyone".

Third Sunday in Ordinary Time

Jesus Preaches God's Jubilee Year

* Nehemiah 8.2-4a, 5-6, 8-10
* Psalm 19
* 1 Corinthians 12.12-30
* Luke 1.1-4; 4.14-21

Each part of Luke's two-volume work (the Gospel of Luke and the Acts of the Apostles) begins with a literary prologue – addressed to Theophilus – following conventions found in historical and biographical writings of the day (cf. Acts 1.1-2).

Like a writer's preface today, prologues indicated something about the author's predecessors; the work's subject matter, plan and arrangement; the author's name and qualifications; and the official addressee(s).

Still, Luke does not tell us his name, mention Jesus by name or indicate the scope of his work. Origen thought that Theophilus, which means 'friend of God,' referred to any reader open to God's message. More likely, however, he was a wealthy Christian who served as the patron for the preparation and publication of Luke-Acts.

The evangelist's statement of purpose speaks of others having tried to give an "orderly account" of the "events that have been fulfilled among us". And it speaks of Luke's own try at an orderly account, so that Theophilus and subsequent readers might know "the truth concerning the things about which you have been instructed". The point Luke stressed about "the truth" may also mean "security" or "assurance" – i.e., something on which one's faith may be safely grounded.

Jesus' synagogue sermon at Nazareth, "where he had been brought up", illustrates how Luke intends us to understand what he had in mind in his prologue. From Mark's Gospel, one of Luke's sources, we learn of the negative response to Jesus' address in Nazareth (Mark 6.1-6a). In Mark's chronology, this visit home took place well after Jesus had begun the Galilean phase of his career.

Luke does not deny Mark's chronology. He even has Jesus expect the townspeople to refer to miracles that he had worked in Capernaum ("Doubtless you will ... say, 'Do here also in your hometown the things that we have heard you did at Capernaum'" [4.23]). But Luke made this episode the frontispiece of Jesus' whole ministry because it manifested key gospel themes, particularly that Jesus fulfills the prophets by evangelizing outcasts and declaring the "year of the Lord's favour".

Leviticus had prescribed, at 50-year intervals, times of "jubilee" when debts would be forgiven and lost land holdings regained by the poor. Isaiah foretold this would be effected by the Spirit working through the coming "Servant of the Lord". Jesus declared that these promises had found their fulfillment "today ... in your hearing".

In the portion of this encounter read next Sunday, Jesus says that God's outreach extends to Gentiles, an assertion that evoked so hostile a reaction from his compatriots that it foreshadowed his death and resurrection. However, God's designs are not thwarted by human resistance. As in the paradox of the Cross, God's compassion – far from being extinguished by hardness in human hearts – continues to spread in ever-widening circles. For God seeks out every human heart "to the ends of the earth" (Acts 1.8).

Rejoicing in God's favour is also a theme in the first reading. Nehemiah described the circumstances of God's people during the Persian Empire's annexation of Israel. The Temple had not yet been rebuilt, the office of king had disappeared and the land was occupied by a foreign power. Only one institution remained that no one could suppress: reading and adhering to God's Torah handed down by Moses.

Celebrating a time of renewal and the birth of 'Judaism', Ezra the priest solemnly proclaimed God's Law. The people were united in their commitment to it. It mattered little that Jerusalem's ramparts had not yet been erected, "for the joy of the Lord is your strength".

The analogy of the body – which is "one" despite its "many" members – was a commonplace in antiquity. Paul used it to challenge the Corinthians to transcend rivalries over which spiritual gifts or offices in the Church were more important. Instead of partiality, each was asked to see that "in the one Spirit we were all baptized into one body ... and we were all made to drink of one Spirit".

Accordingly, "If one member [of Christ's Body] suffers, all suffer together with it". Conversely, "if one member [of the Church] is honoured, all rejoice together with it".

Disciples are asked to express the oneness effected in them, the Body of Christ, by the Holy Spirit. Prompted by the Spirit, Christians encourage each other by sharing each other's hurts and by celebrating each other's blessings.

Fourth Sunday in Ordinary Time

Jesus, Prophet of God's Universal Offer

* Jeremiah 1.4-5, 17-19
* Psalm 71

* 1 Corinthians 12.31–13.13
* Luke 4.21-30

Drawn from an account of Jeremiah's vocation, the first reading tells of his role as "Prophet to the nations". But he expressed awareness that he would be rejected by his own people.

This was the doing of God, who declared, "I for my part have made you today a fortified city, an iron pillar, and a bronze wall, against the whole land – against the kings of Judah, its princes, its priests, and the people of the land".

How could Jeremiah accept this call? Because he had learned to believe in God's word before handing it on. In this regard, there are many points of comparison between Jeremiah and Jesus.

Both had to face hostility from those whom their messages upset. Jeremiah's confidence (like that of the psalmist) parallels Jesus' total trust in his Father ("not my will but yours be done" [Luke 22.42]).

Jeremiah hoped that God would deliver him. And Jesus understood that his Father would rescue him from death. His enemies thought they could silence Jesus for good, but time and again he slipped away from them, as he would definitively do in his risen life (they "led him to the brow of the hill … so that they might hurl him off the cliff. But Jesus passed through the midst of them and went on his way").

In the second half of the Nazareth address, which began with Jesus' proclamation of the Lord's year of favour, he articulated the meaning of his ministry. He was following in the footsteps of Elijah and Elisha, the prophetic servants of God. Like them, Jesus offered God's salvation to outsiders, to foreigners. Paradoxically, Jesus' rejection on the Cross would prove to be a blessing for all the nations of the earth that came to accept the Good News, believe in it and become saved.

Once Jesus began declaring the inclusiveness of God's mercy, the mood of the narrative began shifting quickly. Following the practice of synagogue worship in his day, Jesus rolled up the scroll and handed it back to the attendant. As Jesus sat down to teach, the atmosphere was electric ("the eyes of all were fixed on him").

The citizens of Nazareth heard Jesus' announcement of the fulfillment of Scripture as a promise of special favour for his people and hometown. Still, their question "Is not this Joseph's son?" may be read in a variety of ways ranging from approval to skepticism.

Readers perceive irony in the crowd's reaction, for they know the truth – that Jesus is the Son of God. Even so, Luke observed that "All spoke well of him and were amazed at the gracious words that came from his mouth".

While all were rapt in wonder, Jesus quoted the saying "Doctor, cure yourself!" The proverb makes more sense if "yourself" is taken to refer to Nazareth than to Jesus. Jesus intimated that his townsfolk were eager to share in the blessings that might accrue to a prophet's birthplace, perhaps slightly miffed that he had begun his miracles in Capernaum.

We find Jesus' second proverb about the prophet not acknowledged at home in all the gospels, each time in a slightly different form (Luke 4.24; cf. Mark 6.4; Matthew 13.57; John 4.44). Luke alone introduced the saying with the word "Amen" ("truly"), a word that, in the New Testament, introduces only sayings of Jesus. Along with the Fourth Evangelist's formulation, Luke's version is stated negatively ("no prophet is accepted") and has no exception (Mark and Matthew suggest acceptance of prophets outside their homelands).

The word translated as "hometown" can also mean "home country". Not only will Jesus be rejected in Nazareth; he will also be rejected by his own country and people. But Gentiles will accept him, a point that Jesus underlined.

The manifestation of God's mercy, Jesus asserted, extends from the poor and captive of Israel to Gentiles yearning for God's favour. Precedents for divine outreach to Gentiles, Jesus said, may be found in the careers of Elijah and Elisha. In their ministries many in Israel did not receive God's healing touch, but Gentiles did.

Sadly, because they were not open to sharing God's bounty with others, Jesus' acquaintances and neighbours were unable to receive it themselves. In every age, believers are challenged to grasp the breadth of God's loving plan.

Fifth Sunday in Ordinary Time

Catching People Alive for God

* Isaiah 6.1-2a, 3-8
* Psalm 138
* 1 Corinthians 15.1-11
* Luke 5.1-11

Luke located the disciples' call amid their daily activities. For the tax collector Levi, it happened at his customs table (cf. Luke 5.27-28). For the fishermen Simon and his business partners, Zebedee's sons James and John, the divine summons took place on the lake following a miraculous catch of fish.

As he looked back at the first generation – the apostolic period – Luke was fully aware that the disciples' mission had been entrusted to them by Jesus. Luke knew, as well, that their effectiveness as heralds of the gospel owed more to Jesus' presence at the Apostles' side than it did to their own evangelizing labours.

Accordingly, the evangelist situated his account of the first disciples' call within the overall frame of Jesus' preaching ministry ("the crowd was pressing in on him to hear the word of God"). Simon Peter intuited the power in Jesus' teaching when he replied to Jesus' invitation to lower the nets after a night of fruitless fishing, "if you say so [literally "at your word"], I will let down the nets".

The ensuing catch occasioned a powerful transformation within Simon Peter: "Do not be afraid; from now on you will be catching people". This call was not Peter's alone, but was shared ("When they had brought their boats to shore, they left everything and followed Jesus").

The surface symbolism of Jesus' declaration that the Apostles would henceforth be "catching people", as once they had caught fish, does not seem very promising initially. After all, fish that are caught die in the act of being caught. But we can see another image at work below the surface.

"Catching people" can also mean taking them out of the sea, that place symbolic of control by evil and destructive powers that lurk underwater. In this case, the net in which fish [and people, symbolically] are caught can represent their transfer to another realm.

So, the act of catching people alive for God – even when it is done by Apostles who are sinners ("Go away from me, Lord, for I am a sinful man!") – can intimate that the disciples share in Jesus' liberating activity. It rescues men, women and children from the power of death and introduces them to a new Spirit-inspired assembly, the Church.

Luke, whose account privileges the calls of Simon and several of the apostles, does not give us explicit information about how women became disciples. But he leaves some clues. Readers of the Third Gospel may easily imagine that women followers underwent a type of spiritual experience similar to Simon Peter's as they were being brought to attach themselves to Jesus and his movement.

The story of a woman known as a public sinner illustrates the point. Out of love she washed Jesus' feet, drying them with her hair (7.36-50). Her story, modelling love and forgiveness, precedes Luke's generalizing summary, which tells of women who ministered to Jesus and his associates out of their financial resources (8.1-3). Deep interior movements surfaced feelings of unworthiness; these, in turn, evoked love, forgiveness and a summons to fellowship with Jesus.

Similarly, Isaiah's call made him aware of the distance between his life and the holiness of God ("I am a man of unclean lips, and I live among a people of unclean lips"). God's concern for all people led to the purification of Isaiah's lips ("Now that this has touched your lips, your guilt has departed and your sin is blotted out") – an invitation that Isaiah bring God's healing to others – and Isaiah's generous offer ("Here am I; send me!").

In our day, the Church continues to need men and women to carry on the legacy of the apostolic era by serving as priests and religious. A recent survey of Catholic young people in the United States revealed that many had considered serving God as a brother, sister or priest. But they had been dissuaded from pursuing this path when they encountered resistance from parents or family. When this fact is coupled with the interior, spiritual resistance that typifies most vocations – as the cases of Peter and Isaiah illustrate – today's Church faces a great challenge in helping young people to heed the ministerial vocation: "Come follow me, says the Lord, and I will make you fishers of my people" (Gospel Acclamation verse).

Sixth Sunday in Ordinary Time

Denying the Resurrection Negates the Gospel

* Jeremiah 17.5-8
* Psalm 1
* 1 Corinthians 15.12, 16-20
* Luke 6.17, 20-26

A thin volume by Hans Frör, *You Wretched Corinthians!* (London: SCM Press, 1995) caught my attention when I was working on the ethical dimension of Paul some years ago. The German scholar exposes his interpretation of Paul's teaching by suggesting what the Corinthians might have written the apostle to elicit his responses.

Introducing discussion of the resurrection, Frör imagines one Melas, a representative of Egyptian wisdom, arguing as follows:

> You must make a distinction ... between the earthly Jesus and the Christ who is near to us in the spirit. Jesus, the bodily man, is a part of, an embodiment of, the world which has fallen victim to death. How can divine life have anything in common with decay?

> The spirit is life, Christ in us, infinitely far away from the abyss of rotting bodies and meaningless plagues. Christ, the Spirit, that's eternal life. God's living being, which was there long before the world, untouched by the corruptible. We can experience that. It fills us! Can't you feel it?

Another member of the Corinthian church, Deborah, struggled with Melas' argument and pleaded,

> Tell us what happens to the bodies of the dead if divine life and earthly fate have nothing in common? What happens to the resurrection then?

To which Melas boldly replied,

> Resurrection from the dead? There's no such thing. (p. 74)

In the second century, the apologist Justin Martyr admitted to Trypho the Jew that there are "some who are called Christians who say there is no resurrection of the dead, and that their souls, when they die, are taken to heaven". Justin did not mince his words when attacking such "godless, impious heretics": "Do not imagine that they are Christians".

Paul's answer to some at Corinth who denied the future resurrection of believers was to go back to the foundations of Christian faith — that Christ died and rose "according to the Scriptures".

Paul also argued that underlying this matter was a question about God: "If the dead are not raised" [that is, "if God is unable to raise the dead"] ... then Christ has not been raised, and a whole series of conclusions follows. Among these are that "your faith is futile and you are still in your sins".

For the Christian, everything hinges on Jesus' resurrection. To deny the resurrection of Jesus (or the future resurrection of the believer) is to misrepresent God ("we testified of God that he raised Christ" [v. 15]), to negate the gospel and, ultimately, to empty the gospel of its power.

In a similar way in his teaching, Jeremiah pointed out two different perspectives: one based on faith in God, the other foolishly confiding in human conceptions. The prophet saw and caricatured the contrasting lifestyles found among his contemporaries.

"Cursed", he said, is the foolish person who "trusts in mere mortals and makes mere flesh their strength, whose heart turns away from the Lord". By contrast, he lauded as wise and "blessed" those who placed their trust in the Lord.

The gospel narrative shows how Jesus' preaching (Luke's Sermon on the Plain parallels the Sermon on the Mount in Matthew) exists in continuity with the prophetic tradition exemplified by Jeremiah's preaching. It presents the opening verses of Jesus' inaugural sermon in which the themes of God's predilection for the poor and afflicted and the corresponding danger in wealth recur.

Jesus proclaims four beatitudes and four woes. Three beatitudes say that the afflicted (the poor, the hungry and those who weep) are blessed. Three parallel sayings pronounce woes on those who enjoy the pleasures of this world ("you who are rich", have plenty to eat now or are laughing now).

The distinction Jesus made between rich and poor, full and hungry, laughing and weeping picks up the ancient scriptural doctrine of the two ways. One way, the path of obedient pursuit of God's design for the world, leads to life and blessing. The other way, that of rebellion and resistance to God's decrees, leads to death and curse.

We see this biblical teaching expounded in the first psalm, which acts as a key, interpreting psalmic prayers of every type, indeed every aspect of one's relationship with God. "Blessed is the man who does not follow the advice of the wicked" ... "but whose delight is in the law of the Lord".

Seventh Sunday in Ordinary Time

Resurrection Means Transformation of the Body

* 1 Samuel 26.2, 7-9, 12-13, 22-25
* Psalm 103
* 1 Corinthians 15.45-49
* Luke 6.27-38

Today's second reading picks up Paul's discussion with the Corinthians about the resurrection that began two weeks ago and concludes next week.

The lectionary selections, however, give us only snippets of Paul's argumentation about this important topic. For example, there is a gap of 24 verses from where Paul left off last week (1 Corinthians 15.20) and where his teaching resumes this week (15.45).

In Christ, God has blessed humanity with an anticipation of the resurrection that one day will be shared with the faithful. In his risen state, Jesus dwells in God's presence with a transformed body that is most aptly called "spiritual" – one free of the decay and weakness people experience in this life.

Paul says believers need to see the death and resurrection of every person from God's end-time perspective. He says one can count on Christ's victory over death as a pledge of the future resurrection given all who belong to him (15.20-28).

For if the dead are not raised, Paul argues, the hope he manifests and the suffering he endures each day in his ministry – all of it is pointless (15.29-34). Then Paul replies to the concerns of the Corinthians about the nature of the resurrection, namely what kind of body one should imagine the resurrection body will be (15.35-49).

Here Paul suggests that the best analogy is that of a seed and its transformation into a plant ("God gives it a body just as he has chosen" [15.38]). Like the farmer in the gospel parable who is ignorant of how seeds produce grain (Mark 4.26-28), no one truly knows how the transformation of the body occurs.

No one could have predicted from a seed's appearance what the mature plant's final shape and texture would look like. Just so, only at the final harvest-time will believers be able to fully grasp what the resurrection means for them.

As God's doing, it must necessarily confound present human understandings and all finite imaginings. The truth of what God intends to do for believers at the coming resurrection is summed up in the paradoxical term "spiritual body" (1 Corinthians 15.44).

The seed analogy allows Paul to hold in tension both the notion of continuity between the present mortal bodies that Christians possess and the transformation their bodies will undergo in attaining the resurrected state: "Just as we have borne the image of the one of dust [Adam], we will also bear the image of the one of heaven [Christ]".

A textual variant of this truth declared by Paul turns it into an exhortation: "Let us bear the image of the one from heaven". In this interpretation, Christians are urged to look to the coming one, Jesus Christ, as the grounds for their hope of transformation and make efforts now to conform themselves to the likeness of Christ.

Such hope of future transformation begins to impinge even upon the minds of disciples whenever they struggle to live out the teaching of Jesus. The resumption of Jesus' sermon, which began with beatitudes and woes, challenges disciples to return only good to those who wish or cause them harm: "Love your enemies, do good to those who hate you, bless those who curse you, pray for those who abuse you".

David's non-violence was exemplary, but it did not attain that degree of pardon or love of one's enemies that Jesus espoused. David respected God's consecrated ruler as long as he lived, but after Saul's death took vengeance on the king's family.

The Golden Rule in its positive formulation ("do to others as you would have them do to you") and negative version ("do not do to others ...") was known to Jewish and Greco-Roman societies. In both instances, however, the rule operated within a reciprocal ethic (people do good deeds to others in hope of making friends and receiving benefits in exchange).

Jesus wondered what credit his disciples should expect if they behaved with such motives. But by doing good without expecting return, Jesus' followers would find themselves living like the children of God they are becoming: "you will be children of the Most High; for he is kind to the ungrateful and the wicked". Truly, by fulfilling Jesus' command to "be merciful, just as your Father is merciful", disciples become like God.

First Sunday of Lent

"One Does Not Live by Bread Alone"

* Deuteronomy 26.4-10
* Psalm 91
* Romans 10.8-13
* Luke 4.1-13

Besides fasting and almsgiving, Christian tradition emphasizes greater attention to the life of prayer during Lent. *Lectio divina*, or "holy reading", is particularly appropriate as disciples of Jesus prepare to celebrate the Paschal Mystery – the Lord's Supper, the Commemoration of the Lord's Passion, and the Easter Vigil – with mind and heart renewed by the Lenten observance.

Devotional perusal of the Sunday (or daily) Lenten Scriptures may take a variety of forms. The following pattern, with four phases (reading, meditating, praying, contemplating), is an ancient form dating to medieval times. It is offered as one model that may prove fruitful for followers of Jesus when practised regularly for 20 to 60 minutes at a time.

1. *Reading* reverently the scriptural story of Jesus' temptations takes very little time. However, the first part of *lectio divina* consists in quiet repetitions of the text, savouring its special quality and noting specific features.

In the opening words, the reader learns that Jesus was said both to be "full of the Holy Spirit" and "led by the Spirit in the wilderness, where for forty days he was tempted by the devil". At the end of the 40 days, three of Jesus' temptations were singled out for mention ("command[ing] this stone to become a loaf of bread"; worshipping the devil to receive the glory and power of "all the kingdoms of the world"; and throwing himself down from the Temple pinnacle so that God might rescue him).

In each instance, Jesus refuted the devil with a quotation from the Book of Deuteronomy, a text that Jesus himself must have meditated on often. The narrative concludes by observing that "when the devil had finished every test" (were the three simply typical ones?), he departed from Jesus "until an opportune time" (i.e., the Passion, when "Satan entered into Judas called Iscariot" [22.3]).

Unlike the accounts of Mark and Matthew, Luke said nothing about angels coming to minister to Jesus after the temptations (cf. Mark 1.13; Matthew 4.11). Later, Luke alone noted the presence of a comforting angel during Jesus' Gethsemane prayer (Luke 22.43-44).

2. *Meditating* consists in diligent mental reflection upon the truth hidden in the reading. Some such thoughts might include the fact that, before Jesus, Moses and Elijah had fasted for 40 days at critical periods in their ministry, and that Adam, in Paradise, and Israel, for 40 years in the wilderness, failed the test of temptation and trial, but Jesus did not.

When one attempts to visualize the scene of the temptations, one notes that there is something mystical about the second and third temptations (the devil showed Jesus "in an instant all the kingdoms of the world"; and "the devil placed him on the pinnacle of the temple"). Still, the issues were real. Jesus seized what was at stake, and refused to be taken in.

3. *Praying* means a persevering appeal for divine help in achieving communion with God. It often issues spontaneously from the reading and meditating steps, as persons see their relationship with Jesus or the issues at stake in their lives before God.

What Paul said to the Romans in the second reading – quoting Deuteronomy, as Jesus did – is an apt commentary on this third step of *lectio divina*: "The word is near you, on your lips and in your heart" (cf. Deuteronomy 30.14). Now, the issue becomes one of belief in the heart that moves to expression ("For one believes with the heart and so is justified, and one confesses with the mouth and so is saved"). One prays in one's own words or in a formula such as today's psalm ("Be with me, Lord, when I am in trouble").

4. *Contemplating* may be defined as the fruit of God's compassionate response by which devout hearts raise their gaze to God in sentiments of faith, hope and love. At this point, the disciple of Jesus attempts to speak intimately to God – as to a friend – about the matters pondered in prayer.

Just as the Israelite identified with Israel's history when he and his family came before the Lord at harvest-time ("A wandering Aramean was my ancestor ... The Lord brought us out of Egypt"), so the Christian identifies with Jesus who has won the victory over temptations. The story of Jesus and the Christian gradually become one through prayer.

Second Sunday of Lent

Speaking of Jesus' Departure at Jerusalem

* Genesis 15.5-12, 17-18
* Psalm 27
* Philippians 3.17–4.1
* Luke 9.28b-36

All the scripture readings this Sunday invite the believer to look beyond present circumstances to a hope-filled future being prepared by God.

Having grown old without seeing the fulfillment of God's promise that he would have offspring, Abram brought his complaint before God. The Lord promised Abram that, despite appearances to the contrary, his posterity would be as numerous as the stars in the night sky.

The closing actions of the Abram story depict a covenant-making ceremony. The sacrificial cutting of animals in two indicated that the parties entered into a solemn pledge. Each solemnly bound the other to be willing to die – like the sacrificed animals – if he failed to adhere to the promises made.

Here, however, it was God alone (symbolized by the "smoking fire pot" and "flaming torch" passing between the victims) who made the death-defying commitment. Though "a deep sleep fell upon Abram and a deep and terrifying darkness descended upon him", he received God's offer of land that his progeny would occupy ("To your descendants I give this land").

We learn in the Genesis reading that Abraham (Abram's later name) believed God, "and the Lord reckoned it to him as righteousness". In his epistle to the Romans, Paul described such a trusting disposition as the characteristic of every believer (cf. Romans 1.17).

The gospel, too, depicts an extraordinary vision with divine communication. In a mountaintop locale, "the appearance of Jesus' face changed, and his clothes became dazzling white". The Transfiguration episode on Mount Tabor featured Moses and Elijah talking with Jesus – in the presence of Peter, James and John – about the Greek word *exodos* that he would accomplish in Jerusalem.

Translated weakly as "departure", the term "exodus" encompasses the whole sweep of Jesus' Passion, death, resurrection and Ascension – his crossing over to the Father – what we call "the Paschal Mystery" celebrated every Lent.

The Transfiguration appears in each of the synoptic gospels (Matthew, Mark and Luke) and is referred to by the Second Epistle of Peter ("For he received honour and glory from God the Father when that voice was conveyed to him by the Majestic Glory ... We ourselves heard this voice come from heaven, while we were with him on the holy mountain" [1.17-18]).

Besides giving the topic Jesus was discussing with Moses and Elijah, Luke's account contains several unique features. In words omitted from the first verse by the lectionary ("Now about eight days after these sayings"), Luke linked the story of Jesus' mystical transformation to the first Passion prediction and an invitation to his disciples to take up their crosses daily to follow him (9.22-23). As Luke emphasizes, on this momentous occasion, too, Jesus was praying.

A terrifying experience, about which the disciples "kept silent and in those days told no one any of the things they had seen", the

Transfiguration has been interpreted by the Church as God's way of preparing the disciples for Jesus' death:

> For after he had told the disciples of his coming Death, on the holy mountain he manifested to them his glory, to show, even by the testimony of the law and the prophets, that the Passion leads to the glory of the Resurrection. (Preface of the Second Sunday of Lent)

Luke notes that "Peter and his companions were weighed down by sleep" but that "since they had stayed awake, they saw his glory and the two men who stood with him". These two men – identified as Moses, the founding figure of the nation, and Elijah, the herald of the end-time – testify to Jesus. Though important witnesses, Moses and Elijah are, finally, subordinate to Jesus ("When the voice had spoken, Jesus was found alone").

Peter, James and John had to learn from Jesus a great deal, which they would share later with the Church. They had to listen attentively, for much of what they were hearing was not what they expected. This is why the divine voice offered assurances that what Jesus taught about suffering was pleasing to God ("This is my Son, my Chosen; listen to him!").

Paul noted that Christians could not live "as enemies of the Cross of Christ ... their minds ... set on earthly things". They were to imitate him in his following of Jesus. For true disciples of Jesus there remains a promise of one day sharing his glory ("He will transform the body of our humiliation that it may be conformed to the body of his glory").

Third Sunday of Lent

God Said to Moses, "I Am Who I Am..."

* Exodus 3.1-8a, 13-15
* Psalm 103

* 1 Corinthians 10.1-6, 10-12
* Luke 13.1-9

The Exodus reading describes God's self-revelation in the burning bush, Moses' call and commission, and the way God made known his mysterious Name. It shows how God far transcends our world and yet can be made present on earth.

We see how weak, unworthy human beings can become involved with God's saving plans to rescue those in physical bondage or in physical and spiritual servitude – all who are caught in sin or sinful social structures. God revealed himself as the one God who had been deeply committed to the ancestors of the suffering Israelites.

In answer to Moses' inquiry, God revealed his Name, *Yahweh*, a word that was and remains today very difficult to translate. Some suggest that *Yahweh* means, "I am who I am", or "I will be who I will be", indicating that God cannot be grasped by human categories. Others prefer the meaning "the One who causes to be" – the God who is the origin of all life and all saving activity.

Out of reverence, pious Jews simply wrote the four sacred letters, *YHWH*, without pronouncing the vowels in the divine name, saying instead *Adonai*, "the LORD". To respect Jewish sensibilities, Christians are asked to say "the Lord" when the name *Yahweh* is to be read or spoken in public. Pope Benedict XVI specified that this be the practice in the Catholic Church.

God's relationship to the chosen people of Israel was and remains an elusive presence: burning bush, pillar of cloud by day and pillar of fire by night. What is clear is that God appears in our world to save those he loves. The divine presence became fully manifest in Jesus, who, like the Father, comes to save us by calling us to a change of heart.

In today's gospel, Jesus speaks of two disasters that were in the news during his ministry. Expecting that he would comment, people told Jesus about some Galileans (their neighbours?) killed by Pilate while they were offering their sacrifices in the Temple. Aware that many of his contemporaries would think this implied that these people were being punished by God for some sin, Jesus stated their speculation ("Do you think that ... these Galileans ... were worse sinners than all other Galileans?"), only to deny it outright ("No, I tell you").

Even today, Jesus' teaching that accidents or illnesses are not punishments from God is difficult for some people to accept. While denying that accidents are divine retribution, Jesus drew a lesson from the sudden deaths – a call to repentance: "unless you repent, you will all perish [spiritually] as they did [physically]".

Sudden deaths challenge those who are still alive to reformation of life, coming to terms with their status as sinners loved by God. Biblical teaching asserts that God does not permit accidents to happen to people to punish them for their sins.

According to Jesus' parable, neither does God lie in wait for the sinner to be caught in sin. Instead, the key point of the parable suggests that God, under the image of the owner of the fig tree, is infinitely patient.

A mature fig tree should produce fruit every year, just as human lives should bear the fruits of good deeds. This fig tree had been barren "for three years". Not only did it not bear figs, it seemed to be draining nourishment from the other vineyard plants.

Some human lives seem to produce little, or even to cause damage to others. But like the owner of the garden, God listens to the gardener's appeal for patience with the unproductive (and hurtful) and heeds his suggestion of further treatment ("until I dig around it and put manure on it"). God gives people the time they need.

Still, there will be a day of reckoning and, if a person, instead of bearing fruit, continues in procrastination and non-productivity, he or she must be ready to face the fate of the barren fig tree. Here we find echoes of the warnings Paul noticed in the history of Israel (second reading).

Pilate's malice may have occasioned the deaths of some Galileans, and eighteen people from Jerusalem may have died by chance. But the fig tree (some individuals) will die spiritually because of their inactivity and unresponsiveness to God's appeal made by Jesus and his Church: "unless you repent, you will all perish".

Fourth Sunday of Lent

"This Fellow Welcomes Sinners and Eats with Them"

* Joshua 5.9a, 10-12
* Psalm 34
* 2 Corinthians 5.17-21
* Luke 15.1-3, 11-32

Just as the celebration of Passover marked the beginning of the Exodus, so the celebration of the same feast marked its end ("when the children of Israel were camped in Gilgal they kept the Passover"). Israel's entrance into the Promised Land brought the period of their deliverance from slavery in Egypt to its conclusion.

On the next day, God's gift of "manna" – nourishment for a pilgrim people – ceased. In place of the heaven-sent food, God's people now feasted on "the produce of the land, unleavened cakes and parched grain", foods that could be prepared easily and quickly. The Church has interpreted the Eucharist – Jesus' gift of himself in Holy Communion – as heaven-sent manna, nourishment for the people of God on their journey to the "promised land" of heaven.

Food also plays a prominent role in today's gospel narrative, which begins with the note that Jesus was criticized for welcoming sinners and eating with them. For cultural anthropologists tell us that in the Mediterranean world of Jesus' day, only equals could invite each other to share a meal.

The Pharisees and scribes reproached Jesus for the honour he gave to sinners by eating and drinking with them. A rabbinic tradition held that it was praiseworthy to feed sinners, but eating with them was forbidden. To be the "host" of sinners, as Jesus regularly was, enraged the religious establishment.

In fact, Jesus' reply to the grumbling about his pastoral method began with the parable of a shepherd who had lost one of his hundred sheep, sought it out until he found it and then invited his neighbours to rejoice with him over his successful search.

This parable was followed by its twin tale of a woman who had lost one of her ten coins, swept and cleaned the house until she found it, and then invited friends to rejoice with her. Both parables culminated with Jesus' observation of the greater joy in heaven "over one sinner who repents than over ninety-nine righteous persons who need no repentance".

Both of these brief parables (which are not part of today's gospel reading, but come right before the Prodigal Son story in Luke) pictured God's desire to find sinners and bring them back to the fold, to discover the lost. When sinners turn to God, heaven throws a party; it was this prospect that kept Jesus associating with sinners.

The third parable Jesus told is often entitled "the Prodigal Son". It could just as easily – and perhaps more accurately – be captioned "the Forgiving or Reconciling Father" or "the Two Lost Sons".

While the parable gives a great deal of attention to the younger son, who squandered his inheritance, the closing verses describe the father dealing with the resentment of the elder son, inviting him to join in the feast. Readers are left to judge what they would do in the elder son's place – celebrate his younger brother's reconciliation or stay outside "angry", as the righteous did over Jesus' behaviour.

The younger son acted shamefully in asking for his inheritance, in effect wishing his father were dead. But the elder son also accepted his share and made no effort to reconcile his brother with their father.

When the younger son squandered all he had, he "came to himself", that is, began to repent. His plan was to return as a "hired hand". Perhaps over time he would be able to pay back what he had lost and even care for his father in his old age, as a dutiful son was expected to do.

The father acted totally opposite to what was culturally expected, publicly forgiving his son and healing their broken relationship. The best robe was probably the father's own; it would signify restoration. The signet ring for his wayward son's finger represented enormous trust, and sandals were a sign of the freedom enjoyed by a member of the household, for slaves went barefoot. The killing of the calf – enough to feed over a hundred people – meant the whole village would participate in the reconciliation.

The restoration of broken relationships may be characterized as being found alive ("this son of mine was dead and is alive again; he was lost and is found!"). Or, as St. Paul puts it, reconciliation with God is a "new creation": "see, everything has become new!"

Today's Lenten message, then, is straightforward: "we entreat you on behalf of Christ, be reconciled to God".

Fifth Sunday of Lent

"I Am About to Do a New Thing"

* Isaiah 43.16-21
* Psalm 126
* Philippians 3.8-14
* John 8.1-11

Among all God's saving actions in Israel's favour during the Exodus, the passage through the Red Sea held pride of place and was celebrated in the Song of Moses (Exodus 15.1-18). This song of praise is central to the prayer of Christians in the Great Easter Vigil of Holy Saturday night. In fact, of the nine scriptural lessons appointed for proclamation at the Vigil, it is the only one that may not be omitted.

It is remarkable, then, that God's message in Isaiah foretells a future Exodus (from bondage in the Exile of Babylon) that will be so extraordinary, people will forget the earlier one ("Do not remember the former things, or consider the things of old").

Through the prophet, God foretold an imminent renewal of his saving power surpassing even the events in the desert wanderings ("I am about to do a new thing ... I will make a way in the wilderness and rivers in the desert").

God expressed intentions to reshape his chosen ones so that they would magnify his glory anew ("to give drink to my chosen people, the people whom I formed for myself so that they might declare my praise").

Newness of life is also the gift on offer from Jesus in today's gospel. The story of the woman taken in adultery reveals both Jesus' compassion towards sinners ("Neither do I condemn you") and rejection of sin ("Go your way, and from now on do not sin again").

In an amazing way, Jesus' Spirit-inspired answer to the trap set by the religious leaders saved him from condemnation as a false prophet and denunciation to Roman authorities as a rebel. For, if Jesus had urged that the woman be released, he would have violated the Mosaic law, been reckoned irreligious, and forfeited the titles of prophet and teacher. On the other hand, had he judged that the sinful woman should be stoned, he would have gotten into trouble with the Roman authorities, who had taken the right of capital punishment away from the Jews of his day.

In setting a trap for Jesus, the scribes and Pharisees committed a number of irregularities themselves. They declared to Jesus that "this woman was caught in the very act of committing adultery", yet they provided no witnesses to sustain their case. Thus, Jesus did not have the necessary information to adjudicate the issue correctly.

Jesus' challengers spoke as if the law required the death penalty only for adulterous women ("Moses commanded us to stone such women"). However, Mosaic legislation prescribed the death penalty for both the man and the woman involved in adultery (cf. Leviticus 20.10; Deuteronomy 22.22). Clearly, the woman and the legal issue were only foils for his enemies' intent to entrap Jesus.

Jesus' reaction to the dilemma placed before him seems to be one of disengagement. He stooped down to write in the dirt, an action he would repeat after his reply ("And once again Jesus bent down and wrote on the ground").

Much has been made of what Jesus wrote, including one tradition represented by the textual variant given by the New Revised Standard Version editors at the end of verse 8 ("the sins of each of them"). All of this is mere speculation and detracts from the power of Jesus' invitation to his interlocutors: "Let anyone among you who is without sin be the first to throw a stone at her".

Jesus offered all his conversation partners an opportunity to begin anew. He offered the woman a chance to embrace a new future, no longer as a condemned woman but as a free woman. To the religious authorities, Jesus offered them the category of compassion to judge future cases, instead of the narrow category of control that had motivated their earlier, distorted zeal for fulfilling the law.

Paul saw the resurrection as the only source of true freedom for disciples. Earlier, he had prized righteousness gained from observing the law as a good Pharisee. But having come to know the righteousness that comes "from God based on faith", his outlook was transformed, made new: "I have suffered the loss of all things, and I regard them as rubbish, in order that I may gain Christ and be found in him".

Palm Sunday of the Lord's Passion

"Into Your Hands I Commend My Spirit"

* Luke 19.28-40
* Isaiah 50.4-7
* Psalm 22
* Philippians 2.6-11
* Luke 22.14–23.56

All of Lent is oriented to the Paschal Triduum, the three-day solemn observance of Holy Thursday, Good Friday and the Easter Vigil. Passion or Palm Sunday anticipates the pathos of Jesus' suffering and death, while the triumphal entry into Jerusalem in the processional entrance to the liturgy foretells the glorification of Christ's resurrection.

One of Isaiah's 'Suffering Servant' poems and Psalm 22, with their eerie evocations of the Passion, illustrate the overarching Lukan theme that it was "necessary [that is, was the divine will] that the Messiah should suffer these things and then enter into his glory" (24.26).

Paul's letter to the Philippians likely quotes an early Christian hymn about Christ Jesus' act of emptying himself of equality with God by his obedience to God's plan that led to a shameful death on the Cross. This, Paul claims, merited God's response of raising him from the dead, highly exalting him above all creation.

The consequence of this earth-shattering event is the world's coming to know, through proclamation of the gospel, of God's design that, at every mention of the name of Jesus, "every knee should bend, in heaven, on earth and under the earth, and every tongue should confess that Jesus Christ is Lord, to the glory of God the Father".

Each evangelist, while making use of ancient Christian traditions concerning the last hours of Jesus, quotes the Scriptures to give to these moments his own reflections on these pivotal moments of salvation history.

Satan, who had left Jesus at the end of the temptations, returns to the conflict of his last days by entering into Judas Iscariot (22.3), who would soon betray him. Then Jesus sends Peter and John to prepare the Upper Room for the Passover meal (22.7-13), which he "eagerly desired to eat" before his death. This is the beginning of extended table talk with the disciples, constituting a farewell discourse that includes the disciples' dispute about greatness and Jesus' prayer for Simon Peter to "strengthen your brothers" (22.15-34).

A feature peculiar to Luke's account is the description of Jesus' prayer on the Mount of Olives, which does not have the threefold pattern found in Mark and Matthew, but instead gets supported by a comforting angel. Luke notes that, in his anguish, Jesus "prayed more earnestly such that his sweat became like great drops of blood falling down on the ground" (22.43-44). The text-critical status of these two verses is disputed, with some text critics arguing they were added into some manuscripts later, with other scholars taking the opposite tack, saying that they were removed.

Luke seems to have had special insider knowledge of the interests of Herod Antipas and members of his court (cf. his reference to "Joanna, the wife of Herod's steward Chuza", who was among the women who cared for Jesus and his disciples out of their means in Luke 8.3, and his remarks about Herod's perplexity about, and desire to see, Jesus in 9.7-9). Now, in Jerusalem, after Pilate had twice found Jesus innocent and was trying to cope with the pressures of a mob, Herod receives Jesus from the Roman Prefect (23.6-12).

Herod, away from his realm in Galilee, chooses not to engage himself in the case because he is disappointed that Jesus would work no miracle for him. Herod joins in the mockery his soldiers visited on Jesus and sends him back to Pilate. Through this gesture Herod and Pilate, who had been enemies, became friends, paradoxically agreeing that Jesus was innocent of political charges trumped up against him (23.15).

Journeying to the Cross and mounted upon it, Jesus brings consolation and reward to those who turn to him. He comforts the women of Jerusalem (23.27-31) and welcomes one of the convicted criminals, who turned to him in repentance, to share Paradise with him "today" (23.39-43). As elsewhere in Luke's Gospel, men and women were paired as representatives bearing witness to the kingdom (cf. the man planting a mustard seed and the woman who mixed leaven in meal as protagonists of the kingdom [13.18-21], or the shepherd seeking out and finding his lost sheep and the woman sweeping her house until she finds her lost coin, as images of God's search for the lost [15.1-10]); so, in his final gestures, Jesus reaches out to needy women and men with good news.

On the Cross, Jesus shows profound understanding of human frailty, praying for God's forgiveness for faults committed out of ignorant human weakness ("Father, forgive them; for they do not know what they are doing" [23.34]).

As well, Jesus' final prayer on the Cross differs from the anguished cry of dereliction of the accounts found in Mark 15.34 and Matthew 27.46. Instead of manifesting turmoil, Jesus confidently entrusts himself to God, saying, "Father, into your hands I commend my spirit," words that echo those of the psalmist (Psalm 31.5).

The Resurrection of the Lord: Easter Sunday

"Why Do You Look for the Living Among the Dead?"

* Acts 10.34a, 37-43
* Psalm 118
* Colossians 3.1-4 or 1 Corinthians 5.6b-8
* John 20.1-18 or Luke 24.1-12; at an afternoon Mass, Luke 24.13-35 is an option

Though the first reading is always taken from the Acts of the Apostles – Peter's summary of the post-resurrection experiences of the apostles – the other scriptural readings for Easter Sunday allow a variety of possibilities.

The epistle reading may be the text from Colossians, which invites believers raised with Christ in baptism to "Set your minds on things that are above, not on things that are on earth". For already, in a manner that may only be apprehended by faith, Christians share the hidden life that Jesus, since his glorification in the completion of the Paschal Mystery, enjoys with God in heaven.

Alternatively, the second reading may be the striking passage from First Corinthians, which proclaims that Christ, the paschal lamb of Christians, has been sacrificed. This calls disciples to a whole new way of keeping the Christian feast of *Passover*, that is, "with the unleavened bread of sincerity and truth". (While in English, the name of our religious festival "Easter" comes from the name of the Germanic goddess of spring, other languages preserve a link with the Jewish feast of *Pesach*, e.g. French *Pâques*, Italian *Pasqua*.)

The original participants in the Exodus "Passover" were told to remove all leaven from their homes. Subsequently, among Jewish people, a meticulous ritual evolved to systematically root out everything leavened. Somehow, from this custom, leaven came to represent false teaching or wicked conduct.

For Paul, the implications of the sacrifice of God's Son at the feast of Passover – whose death effected the forgiveness of sins – leads to consequences in the lives of disciples. Each Christian must, after undergoing baptism, which associates them with Christ's death and resurrection, commit himself or herself to living a life of upright conduct.

On Easter morning, the gospel may be one of two gospel passages: John's account of Mary Magdalene's encounter with the Risen Lord, whom she initially mistook for the gardener (20.1-18) or the reading from the Easter Vigil [this year, Luke 24.1-12], as is indicated in a Lectionary note immediately following the Alleluia verse. At a Mass later in the day – on Sunday afternoon – the Emmaus episode (Luke 24.13-35) may be chosen.

Since the Road to Emmaus text is featured on the Third Sunday of Easter in Year A, discussion of that passage is found in *Living God's Word: Reflections on the Sunday Readings for Year A* (pages 78–80). Here, we will look briefly at the passage from John's Gospel and then at the passage from the Easter Vigil.

All the resurrection accounts hint at the reversal of the tragedy of Jesus' death. The ritual of mourning and acts of respect towards the body of Jesus carried out by several faithful women turns to perplexity when they discover the empty tomb, then amazement at the angelic message and, finally, overwhelming joy when at last Jesus comes to meet them.

The Fourth Evangelist suggests what this encounter means for each believer by elaborating on Mary Magdalene's meeting with Jesus. We see the risen Lord as both different from the one Mary knew (she thought he was the gardener), yet the same person who knows her by name ("Mary!"). Jesus tells Mary that now she and others share a new relationship with God, who has become "my Father and your [plural] Father ... my God and your God". Jesus commissions Mary as the 'apostle [one sent] to the apostles', to bring the good news of the resurrection to all the world.

In Luke's account, the message of the angels to the women takes on a particular tone: "Why do you look for the living among the dead?" There is an incompatibility now between Jesus and death. He shares eternal life with God and offers it to those who believe.

Then the angel reminds them that Jesus taught the divine necessity of his suffering ("Remember how he told you, while he was still in Galilee, that the Son of Man must be handed over to sinners, and be crucified, and on the third day rise again").

The promise of God's power has been realized, but the story appears unbelievable to the disciples, who probably thought the resurrection would come at the end-time. Peter, however, is unsure, for he has learned that Jesus' surprising sayings come true. He marvels at the linen grave cloths but does not yet come to faith. That must await his personal encounter with the Risen One.

Second Sunday of Easter

"I Am the First and the Last, and the Living One"

* Acts 5.12-16
* Psalm 118
* Revelation 1.9-11a, 12-13, 17-19
* John 20.19-31

The character of the Second Sunday of Easter derives from the invariable selection of Jesus' two appearances to the apostles, one without and one with Thomas present, as the gospel of the day. The risen Christ shares with his apostles the mandate he received from the Father to go into the world with the message of salvation ("as the Father has sent me, so I send you").

Breathing on them the Holy Spirit (a text that shows the link between the resurrection and the gift of the Holy Spirit), Jesus missions his disciples to set people free ("Receive the Holy Spirit. If you forgive the sins of any, they are forgiven them; if you retain the sins of any, they are retained").

Thomas cannot accept the Good News about Jesus' resurrection on the basis of others' reports and says so, explicitly demanding proof of the convictions he holds, that Jesus was wounded in his hands by nails at the crucifixion and in his side by a thrust from the soldier's lance.

The risen Lord, still marked in his hands and side by the tokens of his Passion (though we should understand them as somehow transformed, too, by the reality of the resurrection), invites Thomas to touch the wounds, to surrender his doubts and become a believer.

We do not know whether Thomas touched the wounds of Jesus or not; the text does not tell us about that, but only of Thomas's coming to faith. In reply to his invitation, Thomas makes the great confession of Jesus' lordship over his life, one that disciples throughout the ages have made their own: "My Lord and my God!"

Jesus then pronounced the deep happiness of disciples who have lived since the exaltation of Christ and believe him to be "the Christ, the Son of God", though they have no visible proofs to fall back on: "Blessed are those who have not seen and yet have come to believe".

The risen Lord's appearance on the eighth day, like Easter itself a Sunday ("the first day of the week"), helped shape Christian conviction that this day should replace the venerable Sabbath (the seventh day of the week) as "the Lord's Day".

In the passage from the Book of Revelation, the source of the second reading throughout Eastertide this year, John tells of a mystical insight he experienced when he "was in the spirit on the Lord's day". It was a vision of the glorified Christ present within the Church ("I saw seven golden lampstands, and in the midst of the lampstands I saw one like the Son of Man").

This symbolic representation of Christ in glory begins with a description of his priestly ("long robe") and kingly functions ("with a golden sash across his chest").

The rest of the visionary representation (vv. 14-16), richly evocative of Old Testament images of God and the Messiah – "His head and his hair were white as white wool, white as snow" [symbolizing eternal wisdom]; "his eyes were like a flame of fire" [omniscience];

"his feet were like burnished bronze, refined as in a furnace" [divine steadfastness], and "his voice was like the sound of many waters" [power and might]; "in his right hand he held seven stars, and from his mouth came a sharp two-edged sword, and his face was like the sun shining with full force" [divinity]) – prepares for the seer's awe-inspired reverence ("I fell at his feet as though dead").

As the risen Jesus had comforted his frightened disciples ("Peace be with you"), so the glorified Christ offers reassurance: "Do not be afraid". Though John's community was undergoing suffering (I "share with you ... the persecution and the kingdom and the patient endurance"), the Son of Man makes three claims: that he is divine ("I am the first and the last, and the living one"); that he is Jesus ("I was dead, but see, I am alive forever and ever"); and that he is more powerful than all the Church's enemies ("I have the keys of Death and of Hades").

Though the risen and exalted Jesus has returned to the Father, he has not abandoned his Church, but remains close to his followers for all time. This is the ongoing message of the resurrection.

Third Sunday of Easter

"Joy Comes with the Morning"

* Acts 5.28-32, 40b-41
* Psalm 30
* Revelation 5.11-14
* John 21.1-19

Today's psalm responsory is taken from Psalm 30, an individual's thanksgiving to God for rescue from some life-threatening experience, possibly a major illness. But the superscription, probably attached much later, attributes it to David and describes it as "a song at the dedication of the temple".

We see here how an individual's prayer – predominantly praise for personal deliverance – is applied to a communal situation. This helps one see how Scripture composed in another context can fittingly be applied to new circumstances. Reference in the psalm to the person having come very close to death, then recovering ("O Lord, you brought up my soul from Sheol, restored me to life from among those gone down to the Pit"), gets applied, by the Church's use in the Easter season, to Christ's resurrection.

The dynamic movement of the poem, as in many other psalms, is from the individual's experience to the community's. The psalmist invites others to share his prayer of gratitude: "Sing praises to the Lord, O you his faithful ones, and give thanks to his holy name". The affliction is seen to have been a temporary one, just as Christ's death was immediately followed by his resurrection ("Weeping may linger for the night, but joy comes with the morning").

The transition from mourning to rejoicing is a sub-theme of the story of Jesus' encounter with seven disciples on the shore of the Sea of Galilee, also known as the Sea of Tiberias, after the major city on the lake. It is found in the dialogue between Jesus and Peter over the latter's love for his Lord. Readers have found Jesus' three questions – "Do you love me [more than these]?" – as opportunities for Peter to undo his three denials.

Earlier, at the Last Supper, Peter had boasted to Jesus that he was ready "more than these" to lay down his life for Jesus (John 13.37). On the night when Jesus was handed over, Peter denied Jesus three times near a charcoal fire (18.18). Now, near another charcoal fire (21.9), Peter affirms his love for Jesus without comparing himself to the others ("Lord, you know everything; you know that I love you").

The rehabilitation of Peter touches on his personal relationship with Jesus, but Christ decides that their relationship will touch many others: "Feed my lambs ... tend my sheep ... feed my sheep". There is a sense that the abundant love of Jesus and Peter for each other overflows to embrace many others.

This theme of superabundance typifies the miracles Jesus worked in Galilee and, in the case of the great catch of fish, became the catalyst for the beloved disciple's recognition of Jesus ("It is the Lord!")

At the beginning of Jesus' ministry, the miracle at Cana – of water transformed into wine – caused the disciples to see Jesus' glory

(John 2.1-11). As well, the miracle of the multiplication of five barley loaves and two fish (6.1-14) to feed a crowd of five thousand evokes the declaration by the evangelist that "from his fullness we have all received, grace upon grace" (1.16).

To a Lord who is so lavish, Peter responds with willing acceptance of the call to pasture Christ's flock. He even willingly receives Jesus' prediction that he will glorify God by his coming death.

Commentators have puzzled over the number of fish caught: 153. While some say it is a recollection of an eyewitness who counted them, Augustine is one of many interpreters who read the number symbolically. He noted that 153 is the sum of all the integers between one and seventeen, and so suggests completeness, the totality of the Church.

The symbolic tie between the miraculous catch of fish and the mission of the disciples is underlined by the words used to describe Peter's hauling in the net. The verb "to haul" is the same one used in 6.44 to describe those God brings to Jesus ("No one can come to me unless *drawn* by the Father who sent me") and in 12.32 to speak of the saving effects of Jesus' death ("And I, when I am lifted up from the earth, will *draw* all people to myself").

The verb hints that the disciples join God and Jesus himself in drawing people into the presence of Jesus. The catch of fish extends God's and Jesus' work into the disciples' lives and the Church's mission.

Fourth Sunday of Easter

The Lamb Has Become a Shepherd

* Acts 13.14, 43-52
* Psalm 100
* Revelation 7.9, 14b-17
* John 10.27-30

The reading from Revelation (the Apocalypse) develops the thought of last Sunday's reading. There we discovered that God's strength was manifest in Christ's death on the Cross and his glorious resurrection.

God's power, the lion from the tribe of Judah, was revealed in the lamb that was slaughtered and now stands in triumph. Today, we learn that Jesus' foremost disciples are the martyrs. Like their Lord, they have won the victory by suffering death rather than by inflicting hurt.

The Apocalypse uses an abundance of images to communicate its startling truths. The triumph of the martyrs in heaven is described as a perpetual feast of tabernacles ("with palm branches in their hands"). This was the joyous autumn festival when Israel recalled the simplicity and joy of living intimately with God in the wilderness. We might imagine it as an ongoing – but not boring – celebration of Christmas or Easter.

The images of victory are also paradoxical: "they have washed their robes and made them white in the blood of the Lamb". For Christian life is a paradox. Those in heaven are there because they followed Jesus in every aspect of life. They gave themselves fully to him, even to death. A living faith that possesses a disciple fully, not just a part of one's being, leads to one's wearing the white robe of victory.

The heavenly vision cites several texts from Isaiah (49.10; 25.8) that referred to Israel's return from exile as fulfilled in heaven ("They will hunger no more, and thirst no more ... God will wipe away every tear from their eyes").

All human hopes are fulfilled in the shepherding by the Lamb. In another paradox, the Lamb has become the shepherd of the sheep.

Jesus as the Good Shepherd is always a theme of the Fourth Sunday of Easter. In today's gospel, Jesus stresses that he and the Father work together in the work of keeping safe the sheep entrusted to his care ("The Father and I are one"). This is the reason why he can say that no one can rob him of his sheep ("No one will snatch them out of my hand").

The Father is greater than any power in the universe, even sin and death. So nothing can break the hold on the sheep that the Father has ("What my Father has given me is greater than all else, and no one can snatch it out of the Father's hand").

The Father and Jesus work together for the salvation of the world, for the sheep of the flock. They are one in this and no power can thwart God's saving plan being worked out by Jesus, the Good Shepherd. What must always be kept in mind is that this saving design is accomplished through a relationship of great intimacy between Jesus and his disciples, the sheep of his flock ("I give them eternal life, and they will never perish"). It is an intimacy akin to Jesus' intimacy with the Father, always open to hearing the Father's will ("My sheep hear my voice. I know them, and they follow me").

Known as Good Shepherd Sunday – since the gospel is always taken from the tenth chapter of St. John – for more than 50 years now, the Fourth Sunday of Easter has been designated by the Church as a day of prayer for priestly and religious vocations. It stresses the shepherding of the flock of Christ and is also a day on which the Church prays for vocations to the ministerial priesthood: shepherds who in our day will carry out the ministry of proclaiming the gospel of Jesus Christ with joy.

In the first reading, we see Paul and Barnabas doing just this in Pisidian Antioch (the Antioch in Turkey, as distinguished from Antioch on the Orontes River in Syria), the Church base from which they began their missionary voyage. There they proclaimed the gospel of Jesus to Jews and Gentiles.

The early preaching of the gospel met with resistance and persecution. Today it is more likely to meet with indifference. The Church needs to be open to the Spirit to find new and creative ways to proclaim God's love for the world made known in the death and resurrection of Jesus, so that today, as in the past, people may be glad and praise the word of the Lord. As today's Psalm expresses it, "For the Lord is good; his steadfast love endures forever, and his faithfulness to all generations".

Fifth Sunday of Easter

God Opens a Door of Faith

* Acts 14.21b-27
* Psalm 145
* Revelation 21.1-5a
* John 13.31-33a, 34-35

There's an adage that God never closes one door without opening another. I do not know its origin, but its intent is to give people hope. The door God opens, bringing joy and confidence to Christians, is a theme of today's liturgy.

This is obviously the case in the first reading, from Acts. It is an account of the completion of the first missionary voyage mandated by the church of Syrian Antioch (13.1–14.28). The evangelist Luke summed up what happened through the ministry of Paul and Barnabas on this first evangelizing tour – "all that God had done with them" – in the following terms: God "had opened a door of faith for the Gentiles".

The missionary commission had been given by the Holy Spirit to Barnabas and Saul (Paul), who were accompanied initially by John Mark, Barnabas' cousin. They went first to Cyprus, Barnabas' homeland, then to the province of Asia Minor, where John Mark left them (13.13). Later this would become a source of friction between Paul and Barnabas, as they disagreed over the suitability of taking John Mark along on the second missionary voyage (cf. 15.36-40).

From their arrival in what is today southwest Turkey, Paul's name comes to the fore in the narrative, henceforth always being mentioned before that of Barnabas. Together they journeyed from Pisidian Antioch to Iconium, Lystra and Derbe, gaining in the synagogues of the region many converts to faith that Jesus was the Messiah. The new adherents came from among Jews and proselytes, Gentile believers in God who, though sympathetic to Judaism, had not fully embraced Judaism for family or social reasons.

The fact that Jews and proselytes attached to synagogues had been grounded in the study of the Scriptures probably explains how the apostles were able to establish leaders for the faith community so quickly from among their new converts. "And after they had appointed elders for them in each Church, with prayer and fasting they entrusted them to the Lord in whom they had come to believe".

Messianic expectation was high among Jews who lived in the Jewish diaspora. The Holy Spirit led some of these to be convinced, by the preaching of a former persecutor of the Church, that Jesus had been raised from the dead and was indeed God's anointed one. Jesus' life and ministry, seemingly called into question by the crucifixion, had been vindicated by his resurrection.

The sufferings the neophytes were experiencing for faith in Jesus' identity as messiah were interpreted as their share in God's will for them as disciples ("It is through many persecutions that we must enter the kingdom of God").

The imagery of heaven that caps the Book of Revelation this Sunday and next began with John, the seer of Patmos, gazing into the world to come and being invited to cross a heavenly threshold: "After this I looked, and there in heaven a door stood open!" (4.1).

One might say that the last chapters of the Bible (Revelation 21–22) are the antithesis of its opening chapters (Genesis 1–3). In Genesis, Paradise is lost; in God's end-time design, Paradise is regained. "Then I [John] saw a new heaven and a new earth; for the first heaven and the first earth had passed away, and the sea was no more". In Revelation 13.1, a great beast had come from the sea, but now no harm can come to those in heaven.

In the end, when God's saving plan is fully realized, God dwells intimately with his people. There is no more crying, pain or tears. Though life on earth may resemble a vale of tears, heaven finds God wiping away every tear from human eyes.

"Death will be no more; mourning and crying and pain will be no more". The new creation has been finally realized ("See, I am making all things new").

Jesus' farewell address reveals his heart. 'Having loved his own who were in the world", we are told that Jesus loved them "to the end" or, to use a better translation, "completely". Jesus interprets his death on the Cross as God's glorification.

The new reality effected through his love is summarized by the Fourth Evangelist not as a new covenant but as a "new commandment, that you love one another". Finally, we see, love is the door to fully understanding Jesus' self-offering.

Sixth Sunday of Easter

"The Holy Spirit Will Teach You Everything"

* Acts 15.1-2, 22-29
* Psalm 67
* Revelation 21.10-14, 22-23
* John 14.23-29

As the Easter season draws to a close, the focus shifts from the Risen Lord Jesus to the Holy Spirit who will come upon the Church at Pentecost. In the gospel, Jesus speaks of the imminent coming of the Advocate, the Holy Spirit, who will "teach you everything, and remind you of all that I have said to you".

However, the Holy Spirit's role of "reminding" disciples of Jesus' teaching should not be understood as simply a case of the Spirit causing the Church to recollect Jesus' words. Rather, it also implies the Holy Spirit's role in assisting the community of the Lord to understand how the teaching of Jesus bears on the new circumstances that surface and need to be addressed as the Church strives to keep alive the memory of Jesus in each generation.

This, in fact, is the Holy Spirit's role at what has been called the Council of Jerusalem. There a debate took place about what was necessary for salvation: namely, whether circumcision and the observance of ritual laws implied by it were prerequisites to belonging to the community of God's elect, or whether faith in Christ and baptism sufficed for salvation.

The first reading, from Acts, gives the gist of the problem and the solution reached, but, unfortunately, none of the discussion of the issue.

Christians who were Pharisees before accepting faith in Jesus insisted that circumcision and following the stipulations of the law were obligatory for Gentile Christian converts.

Addressing the issue, Peter recounted how God had poured out the Holy Spirit on the Gentiles through his ministry, cleansing their hearts by faith. Therefore, he argued, they should no longer be considered unclean or unworthy to enter God's presence in worship, as some Jews were suggesting.

Paul and Barnabas built on Peter's theological principle, relating their experience of the signs and wonders God worked among the Gentiles during their missionary voyage. James, an exemplary Jewish leader, argued that the prophets had foretold what the Church was experiencing: the restoration of Israel (Acts 1–6) and the conversion of the human race to the Lord Jesus (Acts 11–14). So, Christians should put no obstacles to Gentile conversions. All that should be asked for were the compromises needed to enable Christian Jews to participate in table fellowship with non-Jewish Christians.

Three of these concessions to allow people to live in peace involved kosher rules and avoiding meat sacrificed to idols ("that you abstain from what has been sacrificed to idols, and from blood and from what is strangled").

The fourth dealt with illicit sex, "fornication" (in Greek, *porneia*), which has been interpreted in two ways: 1) as avoiding marriages within degrees of kinship forbidden to Jews (taking this view, the New American Bible translates *porneia* as "unlawful marriages"), or 2) as referring to ordinary sexual immorality, for which the pagans were often criticized by Jews in antiquity.

New Testament writings frequently challenged pagan converts to change their sexual behaviour, which included fornication, adultery, prostitution and homosexual practices. Christian morality in the New Testament era was just as countercultural as it is to popular morality today.

The conclusion, then, that circumcision and ritual stipulations such as kosher dietary laws were not obligatory, is announced as the joint achievement of the Holy Spirit and the apostles and elders who had convened ("it has seemed good to the Holy Spirit and to us ..."). When the determination of the Jerusalem gathering was proclaimed in Antioch, church members there "rejoiced at the exhortation" (Acts 15.31).

Periodically in its history, the Church has convened in council – designated as an "ecumenical" or "worldwide" assembly – to invoke the Spirit's guidance in facing new issues that have arisen. The most recent of these was the 21st ecumenical session known as the Second Vatican Council (1962–1965). The Catholic Church's challenge today remains that of correctly implementing the Spirit-inspired decrees of Vatican II.

The glory of the heavenly Jerusalem is the goal of all the Spirit's inspirations. No temple is needed in heaven, for all sacrifices will have ceased. Instead, in heaven there is a direct encounter between the believer and the Lord God Almighty and the Lamb, the Lord Jesus who offers all his peace ("Peace I leave with you; my peace I give to you").

Ascension of the Lord

"You Will Be My Witnesses"

* Acts 1.1-11
* Psalm 47
* Hebrews 9.24-28–10.19-23 or Ephesians 1.17-23
* Luke 24.46-53

Each year, one of the National Evangelization Teams (NET) spends time in several of the parishes in the archdiocese of Ottawa. During their springtime visit, the young men and women of NET, who devote a year or two to spreading the gospel message to younger Catholics, bring a great burst of energy to our ministry to youth.

Some of these junior evangelizers serve after completing high school or a university degree; others after one or more years of college studies. For most it is a life-changing experience.

Through song and mime, group activities and solid teaching of the truths of the faith, NET members give contemporary expression to Jesus' command to the disciples at his Ascension, that "you will be my witnesses ... to the ends of the earth".

As they testify to their knowledge and love of Jesus and their desire to follow his way of life, the fledgling evangelists are strengthened in their own faith. They come away from the year or two of travelling across Canada confirmed in their commitment to the Lord and his Church.

The arrival of the NET van coincides with parish missions for youth or pre-Confirmation retreats and gives our young people a sense of what it might be like to "receive power when the Holy Spirit has come upon you". The young people who take part in the rallies and faith-centred activities invariably speak of their amazement at discovering the happiness that following the Lord can bring to youth just a bit older than themselves.

Each year I enjoy receiving the NET gospellers at my home for early morning Mass, breakfast and high-energy conversation about the blessings of our faith. Though evangelization projects such as this one are rare in the Catholic world, I am pleased that the NET experience, which began in the United States and has branched out to Australia, has grown impressively in Canada and that there are prospects for still further growth.

It would be wonderful if such a process could be developed for other age groups, so that God's design, that "repentance and forgiveness of sins is to be proclaimed in [Jesus Messiah's] name to all nations", might be fulfilled.

Jesus' Ascension ushered in the era of the Church, even if the Eleven Apostles had to wait another ten days in Jerusalem, until

Pentecost, when they would be "clothed with power from on high" with the gift of the Holy Spirit ("what my Father promised").

Henceforth, Jesus abides in God's presence "on our behalf". This intercession for his disciples that Jesus carries on in the Father's presence will last until he "will appear a second time ... to save those who are eagerly waiting for him".

The "salvation" promised in this declaration by the author of Hebrews should be understood as the completion in each person of the saving effects of Jesus' death and resurrection, which have already begun to be worked in the believer through his or her baptism.

The two accounts of Jesus' Ascension, at the close of the Gospel of Luke and as the opening scene of the Acts of the Apostles, look upon this one reality from different perspectives.

At the close of the Third Gospel, the Ascension takes place on the evening of Easter, at Bethany (which was the location of the beginning of Jesus' triumphal entry into Jerusalem). It is described as a simple parting, without the dialogue we find in Acts, and is the prelude to the disciples' returning to the Jerusalem Temple, where the gospel story began with Gabriel's appearance to Zechariah (1.5-23).

This succinct narrative helps the disciples realize that the resurrection and exaltation of Jesus have brought his presence on earth to a joyful conclusion.

Acts informs the reader that Jesus appeared to his disciples for 40 days, a lengthy time in the biblical worldview. So one may conclude that the disciples are ready now to bear testimony about the resurrection and the Good News it implies.

The Mount of Olives, where Ezekiel saw the glory of the Lord rest (Ezekiel 11.23), was a regular place of prayer for Jesus. From there the disciples go to the Upper Room, to pray in their turn and to ready themselves to be witnesses of Jesus to the whole world.

Seventh Sunday of Easter[1]

Yearning for the Glory to Come

* Acts 7.55-60
* Psalm 97
* Revelation 22.12-14, 16-17, 20
* John 17.20-26

Jesus' High Priestly Prayer (John 17) is partitioned as the gospel reading for the Seventh Sunday of Easter in years A (vv. 1-11a), B (vv. 11b-19) and C (vv. 20-26). Thus, this year we read the conclusion to the Farewell Discourse of the Last Supper, which began with the foot-washing and attendant sayings (John 13.1-38) and the major address by Jesus beginning at 14.1.

In prayer, Jesus looks forward to his imminent return to the Father's presence and to a future with his disciples so that they "may be with me where I am, to see my glory, which you have given me because you loved me before the foundation of the world".

Thus, through this prayer, we understand that Jesus, as the Incarnate Logos, simultaneously envisions his union with God before creation and the final era of glory when his disciples will be one in him and the Father ("that they may be one ... I in them and you in me, that they may be completely one").

Jesus began in verse 17.4 by describing his saving work as that of glorifying God ("I glorified you on earth by finishing the work that you gave me to do") and asking the Father to share with Jesus the glory that preceded the Incarnation ("glorify me in your own presence, with the glory that I had in your presence before the world existed").

"Glory", then, refers to the full revelation of God made known in Jesus. Indeed, God's glory links the beginning and end of the Incarnation (cf. John 1.14; 13.31-32; 17.1, 25). Verse 22 of chapter

---

[1] For use in countries and ecclesiastical provinces where the Ascension is celebrated on Thursday.

LIVING GOD'S WORD - YEAR C

17 shows that glory will mark the life of the community of faith ("The glory that you have given me I have given them, so that they may be one, as we are one").

Glory is also a theme in the reading from the Acts of the Apostles. As the deacon Stephen – endowed with a charism that made him a prophet, like Jesus – concludes the longest speech in Acts (7.1-53), a tour de force on salvation history that refutes the charge that he opposes "Moses and God" (6.11), he receives a vision of heaven's glory.

"Filled with the Holy Spirit", Stephen's prophetic consciousness grasps "the glory of God" and "the Son of Man standing at the right hand of God". In this way, Stephen is linked with Abraham, to whom "the God of glory" had appeared, bringing him a promise of divine blessing (7.2).

Stephen is also associated with the death and resurrection of Jesus who, Peter asserted, was "glorified" by the God of the same Abraham (Acts 3.13) and who, in the gospel (Luke 21.27), had said he would return "in a cloud with … great glory".

The assembled council did not have a capital case against Stephen, as he had not blasphemed, but they found a blasphemous case in his claim that the Spirit had led him into God's throne room. Stephen died in imitation of Jesus, asking that this sin not be held against them (Luke 23.34, 46). Still, his prayer is addressed to the glorified Lord Jesus, the one whom Christian martyrs worship.

The Book of Revelation points to the fulfillment of God's purposes. Even if Christians are not completely comfortable with this writing, it brings the New Testament and the Christian Bible to completion. Though our understanding may remain partial and fragmentary (though we have had a chance of delving into it during this Easter season), its message is about God and human history.

Revelation's scope is panoramic and its focus remains fixed on Jesus as the key to understanding God's commands and promises. By meditating on its message, we glimpse what the Spirit is saying to the churches and learn to respond accordingly: "Blessed are those who wash their robes, so that they will have the right to the tree of life and may enter the city by the gates".

The penultimate word is from the one who bears witness (Revelation 1.5; 3.14), who asserts that he comes quickly (22.7, 12; 1.7) – that is, from the glorified Lord Jesus Christ.

The Spirit and the bride now speak together in reply to Jesus. They plead with Jesus to come soon, drawing history to the consummation intended by God. Whether his coming is to be with clouds or as a thief in the night, it will, in the perspective of Revelation, be soon.

The Spirit and the bride make this plea twice, the second time saying, "Let everyone who hears say, 'Come!'" The choral response of Christians is also found in early Church liturgies, such as the *Didache* (*The Teaching of the Twelve Apostles*) and the enigmatic "*Maranatha*" of 1 Corinthians 16.22: "Our Lord, come!"

The Solemnity of Pentecost

"The Spirit of God Dwells in You"

* Acts 2.1-11
* Psalm 104
* Romans 8.8-17
* John 14.15-16, 23b-26

Most challenging among my graduate courses was a tutorial on Paul's epistle to the Romans. Each week I had to translate units of Paul's profound thought on God, Jesus and the Spirit. I was asked by my mentor to include in the 'translation' all the presuppositions and unspoken qualifications needed to express a complete understanding of Paul's theology. To do so I sometimes needed two or three times as many words as there were in the apostle's dense text!

Today's second reading, which describes the dynamics at work when the Spirit of God indwells the Christian, is one of the richest and most complex expressions of Pauline spirituality.

The Greek word (*sarx*) translated by the English "flesh" is a word that has differing connotations – positive and negative – according to the way Paul uses it.

As elsewhere in the New Testament, it can simply stand for the human condition, with its weakness and limitations. St. John uses the term "flesh" to describe God the Son's coming into the world (his "enfleshment" or "incarnation"); "the Word became *flesh* and lived among us" (John 1.14).

Paul uses "flesh" in this neutral sense when he says, "while we live, we are always being given up to death for Jesus' sake, so that the life of Jesus may be made visible in our mortal *flesh*" (2 Corinthians 4.11).

More often in Paul's writings, however, "flesh" connotes that which is apart from God's sphere, something hostile to the realm of the divine. This is the context for the opening words of the reading, which describe people whose mindset is opposed to God: "Those who are in the *flesh* cannot please God". The person whose mind has been renewed by the Holy Spirit, by contrast, seeks above all to live in a way pleasing to God.

Since their baptism, Christians are no longer "in the flesh" in the sense of continuing as sinners rebellious against God. Rather, they have been transferred to the realm of the Spirit, living with a godly mentality as Christ did. "You are not in the flesh; you are in the Spirit, since the Spirit of God dwells in you".

Living in this age, which remains marked with the effects of sin, Christians will continue to feel tension and conflict until their salvation is complete. This will happen only when their bodies get completely transformed into copies of Christ's glorified risen body ("[God] who raised Christ from the dead will give life to your mortal bodies also through his Spirit that dwells in you").

The striking contrasts Paul makes ("dead because of sin" and alive "because of righteousness") refer respectively to the past life of sin, which has been done away with through baptism, and the new life of righteousness that Christ has brought to believers.

Paul uses a wide range of expressions to show that through the saving work of Jesus Christ, the Spirit of God has become the operating principle in Christians' lives, dwelling in them and enabling Christ to be in them ("Christ is in you"). Such a Spirit-led existence lets them experience the guidance of Christ and his Spirit.

Paul's use of the term "debtors" is another way of speaking of the governing principles of one's life. He says that "we are debtors, not to the flesh" without completing his thought (by arguing "we are debtors to God, Christ, the Spirit").

Since "the flesh" (sin-prone human nature at enmity with God) has led to nothing good for humans, they should not live according to its dictates. Becoming debtors to God instead offers Christians abundant life ("if by the Spirit you put to death the deeds of the body, you will live").

Finally, Paul dwells on the freedom of God's Spirit-guided children. Having been enabled to escape the slavery of sin, they enjoy, by adoption, the status of God's children. With Jesus, then, they are able to address God as "Abba! Father!"

This is the full measure of Christian life that Jesus alluded to in saying, "the Advocate, the Holy Spirit ... will teach you everything". It is also the interior expression of the Pentecost experience of "a sound like the rush of a violent wind", "tongues, as of fire", and a community "filled with the Holy Spirit".

The Most Holy Trinity

"Glory to the Father, the Son and the Holy Spirit"

* Proverbs 8.22-31
* Psalm 8
* Romans 5.1-5
* John 16.12-15

In today's gospel, Jesus describes the role of the Holy Spirit in the Church in the following words: "he will guide you into all the truth". The Spirit speaks the truth from Jesus in order to glorify him. Yet all Jesus possessed had come to him from the Father; and Jesus' sole desire was to glorify the Father. In these glimpses into the interior dynamics of God, disciples grasp the selfless life of the Trinity. Each Person of the Trinity is unique; yet each is oriented to the others.

Still, people only know the inner life of God from God's movement towards them in creation (first reading) and in the way they have actually been saved (second reading). Here, again, Christians discover the way in which the Persons of the Trinity selflessly work together "for us men and for our salvation" (Nicene Creed).

Proverbs noted that divine Wisdom was present with God in the creation of the universe, "delighting in the children of Abraham". The sage author of Proverbs issued a plea that humans discover the way to life. Early on, Lady Wisdom preached and uttered prophetic judgments, denouncing folly and uttering scorn against ignorance. But in chapter 8, Wisdom became an evangelist, tenderly pleading her case. Choosing for or against wisdom, in Lady Wisdom's view, is a matter of life and death.

The majesty of creation, which this passage depicts, reaches its climax with the assertion that God delights in being present with his children. Christians may infer that, since this is so, God delights even more in those who have been re-created as the brothers and sisters of Jesus. This came about through Christ's gift of himself on the Cross, a sacrifice out of love for both the Father and for us.

In Romans, Paul told believers that the Spirit makes them fearless in the face of difficulties through the Father's saving activity ("God's love has been poured into our hearts through the Holy Spirit that has been given to us"). The first part of Romans (chapters 1–4) was devoted to showing how, in salvation history, men and women had become alienated from God by the rebellion of sin.

As long as they remained in this condition – which they could do nothing to undo – sufferings and anything that suggested the prospect of death were to be feared. For these brought with them the threats of judgment and condemnation for sin that would follow. Paul brought his history of sin to an end with the Good News that God had done what human beings could not do: reconciled sinful humanity by putting forth Jesus as the expiation of our sins (4.25).

Now Paul turns to the experience of finding peace with God. Because their status as sons and daughters of God comes by faith and through Jesus, Christians can "boast in our hope of sharing the glory of God". Far from fearing suffering, the Christian's daily tribulations lead to an inner transformation of life through sharing in God's life through faith, hope and love.

The Christian's conviction that such hope is not deceptive issues from the Holy Spirit dwelling in the heart of each believer. The dynamic of salvation history reveals the plan by which the Trinity entered into and continues to enter the lives of God's people.

In the Farewell Discourse, Jesus offered his testament to his disciples. He revealed that the Word he spoke to them would serve as the guiding principle for the apostles' and the Church's future. The power of the Word to guide Christian lives is the fruit of the Holy Spirit's work.

The Spirit actualizes (makes real here and now) the Word spoken by Jesus in the past, so that it might be life-giving in the Church. Even the way the Spirit carries out this mission is reminiscent of Jesus. For the Spirit points beyond – to Jesus, just as Jesus always pointed beyond himself to the Father.

And this, paradoxically, is to Jesus' glory, revealing as it does how obedient he was to the Father's will. For the Christian, the way to his or her glory is by way of entering into the dynamic of the Trinity's life so that ultimately God might be "all in all" (1 Corinthians 15.28).

The reason that Wisdom is worth pursuing is that Wisdom is prior to creation, "the decisive act in which the meaning of all God's creative acts is disclosed". God made the universe for Wisdom and with Wisdom as its pattern. It is this truth that Colossians 1.15-16 interprets by seeing in it a description of Christ's activity in creation; other Scripture texts identify Wisdom with the Word ("Logos") of God, with the Law (Sirach 24–28) and with God's Spirit (Exodus

28.3). In the Church's trinitarian understanding of this text, of course, Wisdom is no longer understood as a creature (if, indeed, it was so understood by the Old Testament), but as God's equal, the One who became incarnate and redeemed us by his death on the Cross (cf. the latter parts of the hymn in Colossians 1.15-20), where creation and redemption are linked).

The Most Holy Body and Blood of Christ

Jesus and the Order of Melchizedek

* Genesis 14.18-20
* Psalm 110
* 1 Corinthians 11.23-26
* Luke 9.11b-17

Classical stained glass windows in older Catholic churches regularly portray Melchizedek. This mysterious figure presented to Abraham "bread and wine", sacrificial offerings that anticipate the elements transformed into Christ's body and blood at the Eucharist.

The First Eucharistic Prayer asks God to "be pleased to look upon these offerings (the consecrated bread and wine) with a serene and kindly countenance, and to accept them, as once you were pleased to accept the gifts of your servant Abel the just, the sacrifice of Abraham, our father in faith, and the offering of your high priest Melchizedek, a holy sacrifice, a spotless victim".

Melchizedek's name means "king of righteousness" or "my king is righteousness/salvation". As we encounter him in today's first reading, he held two offices. He was king of Salem, a title interpreted to mean "king of peace" (see Hebrews 7.2), though originally it may have referred to ancient, pre-Davidic Jerusalem.

Melchizedek was also priest of "God Most High, maker of heaven and earth". Carrying out his priestly duties, he blessed Abram (Abraham) as the latter was returning victorious from battling a coalition of city-state chieftains. Abram took joint action with five ancient kings committed to fight four other kings who had plundered the goods of Sodom and Gomorrah and taken captive Abram's nephew Lot, a resident of Sodom.

Later on, Abram would intercede on behalf of Sodom and Gomorrah – cities that are a byword for sinfulness – for the sake of the few righteous folk in them (Genesis 18.22-33). In this earlier episode, Abram risked his life to benefit them. Though Abram's thoughts were focused on gaining back Lot's freedom, in the process he liberated great sinners. Already God's chosen, Abram made common cause with non-Hebrews to undo evil.

Melchizedek brought Abram food and drink, blessing him in the name of God Most High, the Creator. Then Melchizedek blessed Abram's God for delivering him. In response, Abram gave Melchizedek tithes, thereby implicitly recognizing the legitimacy of Melchizedek's priesthood in service of the same God Abram worshipped.

Scriptural mention of Melchizedek includes Psalm 110, a royal psalm, and Hebrews 5–7, in which the sacred author gives his existence a messianic interpretation. Psalm 110, the Old Testament text most cited by the New Testament, calls the ruling Israelite king "a priest forever according to the order of Melchizedek". Ancient readers may have considered Melchizedek to be the precursor of both the priestly and royal lines of Davidic kingship. In this vein, extra-biblical writings describe Melchizedek as the ideal priest-king, with the Dead Sea Scrolls even viewing him as a heavenly judge.

The Epistle to the Hebrews offers an elaborate interpretation of the figure of Melchizedek. In it, Melchizedek is represented as a supernatural figure whose miraculous origin and indestructible life foreshadow the eternal life of the Son of God (5.6, 10; 6.20–7.22). The author of Hebrews was convinced that, through his sacrifice on the Cross, Jesus had shown himself to be God's unique high priest, though he did not belong to a priestly tribe ("it is evident that our

Lord was descended from Judah, and in connection with that tribe Moses said nothing about priests" [7.14]).

In his being, Melchizedek, who was "without father, without mother, without genealogy, having neither beginning of days nor end of life, but resembling the Son of God ... remains a priest forever" (7.3) and foretells the priesthood of Jesus.

In today's gospel, Jesus anticipates his priestly role in the Upper Room and on the Cross. He acted as the liberator of afflicted people, healing "those who needed to be cured" and speaking to the crowds "about the kingdom of God".

Then Jesus performed a great miracle, multiplying five loaves and two fish in order to feed five thousand men. Jesus' gestures ("He looked up to heaven, and blessed and broke them") envisioned the priestly ones he would make at the Last Supper as he gave himself under the forms of bread and wine (cf. Luke 22.19-20).

As Christian disciples gather on the Solemnity of the Most Holy Body and Blood of Christ, they herald Christ's priestly death [and resurrection] until the end of time ("as often as you eat this bread and drink the cup, you proclaim the Lord's death until he comes").

In the Eucharist, Christians share in the sacrificial offering of Jesus, who remains "a priest forever, according to the order of Melchizedek".

Eighth Sunday in Ordinary Time

"A Disciple Is Not Above the Teacher"

* Sirach 27.4-7
* Psalm 92
* 1 Corinthians 15.54-58
* Luke 6.39-45

Many interpreters believe the closing section of his inaugural sermon contains what is distinctive in the teachings of Jesus. Several have been described as 'hard sayings'. It seems that the behaviour Jesus enjoined on his followers was intended to break the cycle of evil actions and reactions found in the world.

The conduct of Jesus' disciples was meant to be so unexpected as to evoke wonderment among others, thereby opening them to what it means to live under God's rule.

In the closing verses of last Sunday's gospel, Jesus asked his disciples to practise a non-judgmental generosity: "Do not judge …; do not condemn …. Forgive and you will be forgiven". When one offers forgiveness to a neighbour, the other is set free of the burden of past hurtful actions. People can begin again on a new footing.

Jesus noted that whoever forgoes recompense and acts generously towards another may count on receiving a superabundant kindness from God: "A good measure, pressed down, shaken together, running over, will be put into your lap". Jesus knows God cannot be outdone in generosity!

In today's gospel, the central importance of Jesus' invitation to love one's enemies is explored from different angles. It begins with a parable that embodies a proverbial saying ("Can a blind person guide a blind person?") The effects of such dependency on one who cannot effectively lead will be disastrous (falling into a pit).

Being blind and trying to lead is like having a beam in one's eye and trying to correct another. Jesus may be suggesting that one is blind until enlightened by a credible teacher. So, one must be attentive and not be led by a blind leader. His teaching about such matters as forgiving one's enemies, lending without hope of return and praying for one's persecutors truly enlightens. These instructions are a sure guide to life.

The teacher–disciple relationship does not consist merely in the imparting of information. Instead, it helps the one learning from the teacher to become what the teacher already is. "A disciple is not above the teacher, but everyone who is fully qualified [that is, after imbibing the teacher's wisdom] will be like their teacher". Disciples are challenged to be like Christ.

The sayings about trees and the fruit they bear makes the obvious connection that fruit can only be as good as the tree that produces it. A good person does good and a wicked person does evil. Links with the previous teaching suggest that the choice of one's teacher will determine what one will produce in one's life.

If one follows the good teaching of Jesus, one will produce good "out of the good treasure of the heart". Jesus' ethical demands are a call to true inner goodness, rooted in the heart, whose natural fruit will be good acts.

The connection of one's good or bad deeds with the heart, the seat of decision making in the ancient world (not the brain, as people think today), is the theme of the first reading, from Sirach. One's speech reveals what is in one's heart: the good one is planning or the evil one is scheming.

According to this wise man from the past, one needs to carefully listen to what someone says before judging him or her ("the kiln tests the potter's vessels; so the test of the just person is in tribulation. Its fruit discloses the cultivation of a tree; so a person's speech discloses the cultivation of the mind"). For the person's words reveal who one truly is ("When a sieve is shaken, the refuse appears; so do one's faults when one speaks").

Eventually, a person's words betray the evil he or she would rather hide. But the art of lying can be great, and words can always mislead. Typically, Ben Sira shows himself prudent and realistic. And he does not always maintain a positive view of his fellows ("Do not praise someone before they speak, for this is the way people are tested").

Taking a different tack than Sirach, Jesus asks his disciples to imagine the possibility of a truly good heart through its being shaped by his wisdom.

In closing his teaching on the resurrection, Paul speaks of God's final victory over sin in the followers of Jesus: "When this perishable body puts on imperishability, and this mortal body puts on immortality".

Ninth Sunday in Ordinary Time

A Centurion's Faith

* 1 Kings 8.41-43
* Psalm 117
* Galatians 1.1-2, 6-10
* Luke 7.1-10

Roman centurions play significant roles in Luke's two-volume work, Luke-Acts. A centurion confessed his righteousness at Jesus' death: "Certainly this man was innocent" (Luke 23.47). In Acts 10.1–11.18, the experience of the centurion Cornelius – upon whose family the Holy Spirit falls – persuades Peter that salvation is offered to Gentiles without their being obliged to assume dietary prescriptions. This is a watershed in salvation history.

In today's gospel reading, a centurion models faith. As the name implies, the centurion commanded one hundred soldiers of the hated occupying Roman power. He was one of 60 centurions whose ranks composed a legion. The centurion had to make provision for his men's well-being, commanding them at their post and in battle. He understood Jesus to be like him as "a man set under authority".

The centurion asked the Jewish elders to intervene with Jesus, about whose healing powers he had heard. Though a member of the hated "enemy" (whom Jesus had earlier commanded his disciples to love), the centurion had shown himself a man worthy of trust because of an unusual regard for the Jewish people, which had led him to contribute personal funds to build the local synagogue.

Jesus readily agreed to go with the emissaries, but as Jesus approached his house, the centurion felt a scruple about inviting a rabbi to enter his Gentile quarters. So he uttered a humble petition – now paraphrased on the lips of communicants in the Eucharistic liturgy – "Lord ... I am not worthy to have you come under my roof .... But only speak the word, and let my servant be healed".

At these words, Jesus expressed amazement and turned his gaze on the crowd, declaring, "I tell you, not even in Israel have I found such faith". Even a Gentile, who had not so much as gazed on Jesus, can manifest a completeness of faith surpassing what one would expect of adherents of the faith community called by God.

The significance of the interaction between Jews and Gentiles was natural to Galilee, which was known as "Galilee of the Nations" because of the widespread contact Jews had with the Gentiles who lived among them or passed through on commercial trade routes. The possibility that Gentiles would be inspired by Jews to come to worship the one God – who is the sole Creator of all and the Redeemer of Israel – and call out to him for mercy is found in today's first reading. It is expressed in the Prayer of Solomon at the dedication of the Jerusalem Temple.

While focused primarily on the needs of Israel, the prayer attains a universal dimension when Solomon imagines a future when foreigners will come to know God and worship at the Temple. Solomon asks that their prayer be heard so that "all the peoples of the earth may know your name and fear you", reverencing the one true God.

The Apostle called to bring to all the nations of the world news of the salvation that God has made available in Christ Jesus introduces himself in the passionate letter to the Galatians, which is read today and for five more weeks. Paul declares himself to be "an apostle – sent ... through Jesus Christ and God the Father, who raised Christ from the dead".

Paul makes it very clear that who he is and what he preaches do not depend on "human beings" and that he eschews any purely human interpretation of Christian life because it can lead away from the grace of the gospel. This falling away from the gospel is what he would spare his converts.

Most striking in the introduction of this epistle is the total absence of any extended note of thanksgiving, which typifies the other Pauline correspondence so as to signal the graces God has given to a particular community and to indicate the challenges to be faced with the divine assistance (cf. 1 Thessalonians 1.2-10; 1 Corinthians 1.4-9; Philippians 1.3-11).

Paul was outraged because he feared that enemies of Christ's gospel were sowing seeds of confusion among the churches of Galatia by suggesting that prescriptions of the law were still in force and that Christians, who had been taught by Paul that they had been set free of these demands, had now to surrender their freedom in Christ for a perverted version of the gospel. Paul insisted that they not buy into such propositions, no matter the source of this teaching, whether it come from an angel or even from himself! For life in Christ is not entered by works of the law, but by the faith that Jesus praised in the centurion.

Tenth Sunday in Ordinary Time

The Widow of Nain Is Blessed

* 1 Kings 17.17-21a, 22-24
* Psalm 30
* Galatians 1.11-19
* Luke 7.11-17

In the inaugural sermon he gave in his hometown of Nazareth, Jesus referred to the widow of Zarephath. He said that, though there were many widows in Israel in his time, Elijah was not sent to any of them but only to a foreign widow (cf. Luke 4.25-26).

In fact, the reference there was to the first of two episodes involving Elijah with the widow and her son (1 Kings 17.8-16), whereas the emphasis today is on the second, equally dramatic episode.

Today's reading from Kings offers a link with the gospel of this Sunday, in that both deal with the raising and restoration to a widow of an only son. In the gospel narrative, the verb Luke uses to refer to Jesus' delivering of the son to his mother is the same one that the Greek version of 1 Kings 17.23 used when informing the reader that Elijah "gave him to his mother". In that story, the son moved from death to life, and his mother moved from a stance of disbelieving hostility to a confession of faith.

Though the gesture of Elijah in restoring life to the widow's son has a quasi-magical aspect, suggesting the transfer of the life force through bodily contact, the real focus falls on the son's movement from death to life. And overall, Elijah's deed is more a matter of prayer than of magical method.

The day after the healing of the centurion's servant (last week's gospel), Jesus and his followers encountered a funeral cortege carrying the deceased only son of a widowed mother. Luke regularly characterized towns as cities (perhaps because his readers were urban dwellers); Nain, which he refers to as a city, barely qualified as a town.

The body of the young man was laid out on a bier – basically a wooden plank – and Jesus, called "the Lord" for the first time by Luke, was moved by compassion and invited the widow to stop weeping. Then, "he touched the pallet", causing the bearers to stop, and called out to the young man that he should arise. Using a term to indicate recovery from an incapacitating injury, the narrative tells us the man began to speak.

The crowd's reaction was one of reverence for God ("Fear seized all of them") and they glorified God – a typical reaction in Luke's Gospel, where the focus regularly moves from Jesus to his Father.

Perhaps noting the link with the story of Elijah and a widow, the bystanders proclaimed that "a great Prophet has risen among us!" and go further with the exclamation "God has looked favourably on his people!" The Lukan narrative suggests that the news of this deed spread widely and came even into the desert prison of Machaerus and the attention of John the Baptist, who inquired about its meaning, asking whether Jesus is a prophet or more. This episode does not feature in this sequence of Sunday lectionary readings as it appeared, drawn from Matthew 11.2-6, on the Third Sunday of Advent in Year A.

Paul's transition from persecutor of the Church to its chief apologist is well known from the three accounts of the "conversion" he underwent on the Damascus Road (Acts 9.1-19; 22.1-21 and 26.2-23). Each of these narratives is a secondary account shaped by Luke for his own purposes.

By contrast, the account Paul gives of his change of orientation in life and perspective is more discreet, invoking the image of his vocation as the call of a prophet: "God, who had set me apart before I was born and called me through his grace, was pleased to reveal his Son to me, so that I might proclaim him to the Gentiles".

Paul maintains, as in last week's selection from Galatians, that the gospel he received came directly from God ("I received it through a revelation of Jesus Christ") and not from a human being.

Paul intimates that it took him time, under the Lord's guidance, to absorb this experience. He did not confer with anyone ("flesh and blood"), nor did he go up to Jerusalem to meet those who were apostles before him. He spent time in "Arabia" – possibly the Nabatean Kingdom south and east of Damascus – to preach the gospel there before returning to Damascus.

Only after several years did Paul make a trip to confer with the apostolic leadership in Jerusalem, who, we learn later in the epistle, acknowledged the grace he had received to go to the Gentiles with the gospel message (Galatians 2.7-10).

Eleventh Sunday in Ordinary Time

"It Is No Longer I Who Live, But ... Christ ... in Me"

* 2 Samuel 12.7-10, 13
* Psalm 32
* Galatians 2.16, 19-21
* Luke 7.36–8.3

All the readings today speak of an inner transformation – a conversion, if you will – that brings about a new interior reality in Paul, David and a sinful woman.

The polemical character of Galatians comes to the fore several verses before today's passage (cf. Galatians 2.11-14). There Paul recounts an episode that took place at Antioch in which Simon Peter (Cephas) had backtracked on table fellowship linking Jewish and Gentile Christians.

When some Judaizers (those who would have Christians embrace Jewish dietary and other legal prescriptions) came to Antioch and criticized the freedom Peter had exercised in eating with Gentile converts, he and Barnabas changed their practice. Paul says that he confronted Peter on this insincere manner of acting.

Since the same issue was unsettling Paul's Galatian converts, he repeated his insistence that one is saved "not by the works of the law" but "through faith in Christ Jesus".

Paul declares that those who continue to insist on observance of the law as a necessary condition for the Gentiles' full sharing in the people of God are, in effect, declaring Christ's death null and void and returning to social and religious norms that defined the status quo before Christ's death.

In his exposition, Paul says that the key reality is that Jesus Christ died "to set us free from the present evil age" (Galatians 1.4). The new life that Jesus inaugurated meant for Paul nothing less than the annihilation of his former identity and way of being: "I have been crucified with Christ, and [now] it is no longer I who live, but it is Christ who lives in me".

Though he lives his life "in the flesh" [with the human weaknesses that that statement underlines], the greater truth to which Paul clings is that "I live by faith in the Son of God, who loved me and gave himself for me". This is the mysticism that Paul taps into elsewhere, where he describes baptism as participation by the believer in the crucifixion, death, burial and resurrection in union with Christ (Romans 6.1-11).

The reading from Second Samuel concludes the prophet Nathan's confrontation with David over the adultery committed with Bathsheba and the murder of her husband, Uriah the Hittite. Nathan had told a parable that enraged David, who shouted out, "the man who has done this deserves to die", to which the prophet replied, "You are the man!" (2 Samuel 12.5-7).

Instead of suffering the death he deserved, David had a change of heart and repented, and God forgave him. We further learn that the sins he committed would have social consequences in David's lifetime and among his posterity, for that is what happens when sin is unleashed in the world.

Still, God's mercy is greater than any sin, as we learn from Jesus' meeting in the gospel with "a woman in the city, who was a sinner". Implied in the dramatic encounter is a contrast between Simon the Pharisee – most likely a devout and upright layman who had a narrow outlook – and the sinful woman whose reception of the forgiveness Jesus bestowed on her evoked a lavish expression of love.

Luke's story has affinities with the anointing of Jesus at Bethany at Passover (Matthew 26.6-13; Mark 14.3-9; John 12.1-8). But it is also very different: the ointment is not described as "pure nard", nor is it used to anoint the head of Jesus as for a king after his triumphal entry into Jerusalem.

Luke's narrative is distinctive because it develops the relationship between forgiveness and love, in the way in which it evokes the character of the woman.

Further, the components of the story are unified: through the anointing along with the Pharisee Simon's reaction (Luke 7.38-39); by the riddle with Simon's answer (vv. 40-43); by Jesus' responses to Simon (vv. 44-47) and to the woman (vv. 48, 50); and by the response of the other guests (v. 49).

Simon thought he was blameless, "knew" that the woman was a sinner and presumed her action had defiled Jesus. But Jesus contrasted the cool hospitality of Simon with the sincere affection shown by the woman.

In the Middle East, the importance of honour and shame cannot be overestimated. So Simon was doubly exposed by the woman's shameful display of affection and by his guest's drawing attention to his limited hospitality.

Jesus' closing remark in the story leaves hearers with a puzzling conundrum: does love lead to forgiveness, or is one's ability to love the outcome of having been forgiven? For believers, as was the case with Paul, David and the woman, if once our lives have been transformed by our experience of God's grace, we can never get over the fact that we have been forgiven.

Twelfth Sunday in Ordinary Time

Jesus' Messianic Agenda: Taking up the Cross Daily

* Zechariah 12.10-11; 13.1
* Psalm 63
* Galatians 3.26-29
* Luke 9.18-24

From Luke we learn that it was Jesus' feeding of the five thousand that led the crowds to suspect that Jesus might be an eschatological figure (that "John the Baptist ... Elijah ... [or] one of the ancient prophets has arisen"). For their part, the disciples – through Peter, their spokesman – confessed their conviction that Jesus was "the Christ of God".

If, as many scholars suspect, Luke was following Mark's storyline in the account of Jesus' early ministry, he has linked the feeding of the crowds with Peter's confession by omitting a major portion of Mark's narrative (6.45–8.26), notably the feeding of the four thousand (8.1-10).

Further, Luke has not chosen to inform his readers that the location of this watershed moment was near "the villages of Caesarea Philippi" (Mark 8.27). Instead, Luke focused on the fact that the dialogue happened "One day when Jesus was praying alone, with only the disciples near him".

Peter's confession was followed by Jesus' command to keep quiet about his identity and by the first prediction that the Son of Man would fulfill his messianic destiny by suffering, dying and rising from the dead on the third day, as in the Gospels of Mark and Matthew.

Still, Luke made no mention of Peter's rebellion against Jesus' teaching or Jesus' subsequent reply, with its rebuke of Peter's too "human" way of thinking (cf. Mark 8.32-33; Matthew 16.22-23). In this way, Luke enhanced the portrait of Peter offered to the Church. When Jesus prayed for Peter in the Passion narrative, he promised that after his conversion, he would strengthen the brethren (Luke 22.31-34).

In Luke's perspective, the rich teaching of Jesus on discipleship served not as a corrective to a mistaken viewpoint, but took its place as the dynamic core of the gospel way leading to eternal life. Five sayings described the demands of being a disciple to Jesus; only two are given in today's gospel reading (Luke 9.23-24), but we shall comment on the others as well (9.25-27).

Everyone who wants to be a follower of Jesus must do so every day. Only Luke describes discipleship as this daily imperative. Indeed, while denying self and taking up the cross appear in the Greek aorist tense (a single definite action), the present imperative of the verb "to follow" should probably be translated as "keep on following me".

The second saying unveils the paradox that lies at the heart of the gospel: "whoever wants to save their life will lose it, and whoever loses their life for my sake will save it". Faced with the option of pursuing Jesus' messianic agenda or indulging one's own interests, Jesus says it is only the former that leads to fulfillment.

The third saying addressed marketplace issues ("What does it profit them if they gain the whole world, but lose or forfeit themselves?"). Here we note that the NRSV plural translation, adopted for the sake of inclusiveness, takes some of the edge off the challenge that Jesus addresses to each person. Jesus contends that there are dimensions of life that are vital to happiness that cannot be satisfied by possessions or wealth.

The fourth saying demands public expression of discipleship, which will be acknowledged at the end of time. Those "ashamed of" Jesus and his words in this life will be ashamed when the Son of Man "comes in glory". The fifth saying assured Jesus' hearers that some present would experience aspects of the coming of God's kingdom, even though its fullness must remain a future hope.

In a text fulfilled in Jesus' piercing on Calvary (cf. John 19.37), Zechariah foresaw a period of mourning in Israel ("as one mourns for an only-begotten son ... as one weeps over a firstborn"). After this period of grief, however, God would provide for the house of David a fountain of cleansing to save people "from sin and impurity".

Paul assured the Galatians – who were tempted to abandon their faith commitment to the gospel of the Cross – that through their baptism they had become a new creation. Henceforth, no distinction (Jew or Greek, slave or free, male or female) would be of any account, "for all of you are one in Christ Jesus".

Thirteenth Sunday in Ordinary Time

Living in the Freedom of Christ

* 1 Kings 19.16b, 19-21
* Psalm 16
* Galatians 5.1, 13-18
* Luke 9.51-62

At the beginning of July, the citizens of Canada and the United States celebrate their national holidays, Canada Day (July 1) and Independence Day (July 4). Authentic patriotism is celebrated. Sentiments of gratitude for present-day freedoms readily come to mind.

In this context, Paul's reminder to the Galatians may seem singularly fitting: "For freedom Christ has set us free"! Apt, too, is his exhortation "Stand firm, therefore, and do not submit again to a yoke of slavery".

As we saw in recent weeks, Galatians deals with the issue of whether Gentile converts are bound to observe Jewish ritual stipulations. Paul's argument was that observance of the law is a quagmire, and so he offered a different approach: "the only thing that counts is faith working [expressing itself] through love" (Galatians 5.6).

For those who would be disciples, the only avenue to a right relationship with God is faith in the saving deed of God who let Jesus die on the Cross for sinners, then raised him from the dead.

At the start of his Travel Narrative (9.51–19.27), Luke noted that Jesus "set his face" to accomplish God's purpose in willing obedience to the Father. In turn, by means of sayings on the cost of being a disciple, Jesus challenged individual persons to enter generously with him into accomplishing God's saving plan.

We learn that the demands of being a disciple of Jesus supersede every other duty – whether care of self, of the dead, or of one's family. Two individuals approached Jesus, volunteering to join his company, while he engaged another with a personal invitation to "Follow me".

The first individual was told that it costs no less than everything to be a close follower of Jesus. The second individual responded to Jesus' call by noting that he was obligated to carry out the sacred familial service of caring for his parents until death. But Jesus' rejoinder was harsh and uncompromising: "Let the dead bury their own dead". Those alive in God's service can get on with a life-giving service to "go and proclaim the kingdom of God".

Jesus' challenge to the third candidate for discipleship bears affinities with Elijah's call of Elisha. Elijah allowed Elisha to act out his change in lifestyle. His actions (killing a yoke of oxen, boiling the animals as a sacrifice and sharing a holy meal) represent separation from his former way of life, thanksgiving to God for new life, and solidarity with people he would henceforth serve as a prophet. Jesus does not even allow a farewell to family!

Paul insists that to help disciples fulfill his earnest demands, the Risen Lord Jesus poured out on them his Holy Spirit. This freely given Spirit now enables believers to do what, on their own, they could not achieve – live the new life of God's favour.

With a renewed vision of God – as the one who freely offers redemption to those who believe – disciples need no longer seek their own personal or religious advantage but that of their neighbour: "through love, become slaves to one another. For the whole law is summed up in a single commandment, 'You shall love your neighbour as yourself'".

If you "live by the Spirit" (that is, walk in the way that the Spirit guides your disciple's life), Paul told the Galatians, you will not carry out the desire of the flesh. "What the flesh desires" refers not only to sexual passions, but to the whole sphere of fallen humanity in its opposition to God. The list of "works of the flesh" in 5.19-21 begins with three instances of sexual misconduct, but gives much more emphasis to other offenses.

"The flesh" stands for any self-seeking human desire opposed to the divine will and the wholeness of community life. Paul's opponents probably stressed the fearsome power of this evil impulse of the flesh and offered "obeying the law" as the way to overcome it. Paul rebutted this claim, declaring that the Spirit of God is the only agent powerful enough to undo the grip of the flesh: "if you are led by the Spirit, you are not subject to the law".

Immediately following the second reading (Galatians 5.19-23), Paul enumerated works of the flesh and fruits of the Spirit. He was acutely aware that in the corporate life of the Church, "the flesh" produces factions and strife. By contrast, the Spirit brings to the faith community love, joy, peace, patience, kindness, generosity, faithfulness, gentleness and self-control. Church members aspire to reflect today these expressions of the freedom Christ makes possible and in this way contribute to the good of their parishes and their countries.

Fourteenth Sunday in Ordinary Time

Jerusalem: City of Joy and Peace

* Isaiah 66.10-14
* Psalm 66
* Galatians 6.14-18
* Luke 10.1-12, 17-20

With the encouragement of Blessed Pope John Paul II and Pope Benedict XVI, the Holy See has continually expressed the wish that Jerusalem might attain special international status as a city of justice, joy and peace.

For Jerusalem is *the* city, dear to the hearts of believers within the three great monotheistic faiths: Judaism, Christianity and Islam. The Catholic Church simply continues to express a hope that extends back to the time of the prophets: "Rejoice with Jerusalem and be glad for her, all you who love her".

Third Isaiah (chapters 56–66) repeated the yearning of his predecessors, striving to offer comfort and hope to the returning exiles faced with a ruined Jerusalem and discouraged by difficulties they were experiencing. There would come a day, Isaiah promised in the Lord's name, when Jerusalem would know peace at last.

Then would Jerusalem be a focal point for the ingathering of Jews dispersed among the nations. It would also radiate peace for all the peoples of the earth. God promises, "I will extend prosperity to her like a river, and the wealth of the nations like an overflowing stream".

Once the exiles had become settled in the land, the prophecy of Isaiah began to acquire an eschatological (end-time) meaning. Christians understood the text to refer to the joy brought by the Good News in the ministry and teaching of Jesus.

All the synoptic gospels depict the mission carried out by the Twelve. During their missionary journey, the Apostles announced the peace of God's kingdom to the towns and villages of Galilee.

Luke alone mentions a second mission, confided by Jesus to 70 (or 72) others, whom the Lord sent out "in pairs to every town and place where he himself intended to go".

Half the New Testament manuscripts list the number of missionaries as 70, while the others read 72. The first group probably reflects the Hebrew text of Genesis 10, which lists 70 nations, whereas the Greek Bible mentions 72. Thus, this mission foreshadows the outreach of the Church to the nations of the world (cf. Luke 24.47).

The messengers were sent "ahead of him" (literally, *before his face*) to prepare the way for Jesus in each village. So these evangelists served as forerunners of Jesus' personal presence. His mission address to them began with two proverbs: "The harvest is plentiful, but the labourers are few ..." and "I am sending you out like lambs into the midst of wolves".

In the Old Testament, the harvest image projected a message of urgency, and therefore suggested God's judgment. People had to make a decision, as they would by accepting or rejecting the message brought by Jesus' envoys. As the natural predator of the lamb, the wolf figure alerted the disciples to the dangers and opposition they would encounter.

In his speech, Jesus also told his disciples to be ready for positive and negative receptions, gave them behavioural procedures on entering houses and towns, and twice declared the heart of the message they would herald in his name: "The kingdom of God has come near to you". The message of Jesus seeks out people of *peace*, as he directs them to "say 'Peace to this house!' ... if someone of peace is there".

Jesus instructed the disciples not to move from house to house, perhaps to prevent them seeking better quarters. His advice to "eat what is set before you" effectively served to break down social and religious barriers. The invitation to "cure the sick" showed that they shared in Jesus' authority and power by caring for people's physical needs.

Any who rejected the message of Jesus invited a public gesture of repudiation ("even the dust of your town that clings to our feet, we wipe off in protest against you"). But this would not invalidate the message that God's reign had broken into the world for people distant from God's blessings.

Jesus' mission sayings challenge the Church in each age to proclaim the gospel boldly. He counselled innocence, sincerity, vulnerability and non-resistance. Above all, Jesus challenged his disciples to a single-minded purpose, to tell of God's condescension in offering the world an extraordinary message of joy and peace.

Once having experienced the power of the gospel through his encounter with the risen Lord, Paul relativized everything else ("neither circumcision nor uncircumcision is anything"). Indeed, a whole new order had come into being: "a new creation is everything!"

Fifteenth Sunday in Ordinary Time

On Being a Neighbour to One in Need

* Deuteronomy 30.10-14
* Psalm 69 or 19
* Colossians 1.15-20
* Luke 10.25-37

The Book of Deuteronomy presents Moses speaking on the threshold of the Promised Land. Giving his final instructions, he begs God's people to be faithful to the Lord's ways. In today's reading, he insists that they listen to and heed – that is, obey – God's Torah by putting it into practice.

Many centuries after Moses, readers of this deeply spiritual book – the one most often cited by Jesus in the New Testament – know that its message is addressed to them. In patiently attending to its message, they come to know they must be totally engaged in carrying out its divinely inspired precepts. For clinging to God's instruction will be the key to happiness ("The precepts of the Lord are right, rejoicing the heart ... More to be desired are they than gold, even much fine gold; sweeter also than honey, and drippings of the honeycomb").

Moses somewhat rhetorically argued that Torah observance did not require one to ascend to the heavens, as Enoch had (Genesis 5.24) or Elijah would (2 Kings 2.1-12). Nor did one have to go across the sea to find it. Instead, in a passage anticipating the prophecies of Jeremiah (31.33) and Ezekiel (36.26-27), which foretell God's Spirit writing Torah on human hearts, Moses argued, "it is in your mouth and in your heart for you to observe".

Moses insisted on God's holy people putting the commandment into practice, pleading it "is not too hard for you".

Luke's depiction of Jesus, which at times likens him to a second or new Moses, stresses the notion of faith in action, putting the emphasis on *doing* ("what must I *do* to inherit eternal life?" ... "*do* this, and you will live" ... "Go and *do* likewise"). Following in the footsteps of Moses, who received and handed on God's Law to Israel, Jesus came to teach it and interpret it.

Though the legal expert ("a lawyer") was considered wise in contemporary society, his motives were not pure (he "stood up to test Jesus"). Yet when Jesus asked him, in turn, how he read the law, he correctly answered, combining Deuteronomy's command of single-minded love of God (Deuteronomy 6.5) with a text from Leviticus (19.18) on love of neighbour – a single commandment in two parts.

The lawyer tried to justify himself in light of Jesus' invitation to keep this double injunction. He asked about the identity of his neighbour. In reply, Jesus told one of the most shocking yet powerful of his parables, about a compassionate Samaritan.

The parable is violent and provocative. One hears with horror of the injuries inflicted on the Jewish traveller: he "fell into the hands of robbers, who stripped him, beat him, and went away, leaving him half dead". Perhaps more shocking was the behaviour of observant Jews whose consideration of their own safety or concern for ritual purity (a corpse defiled the one who touched it) could lead them to pass by "on the other side".

For Jews, caring for one's neighbour meant first of all looking after one's fellow Israelite. But "a priest" and "a Levite" could not be bothered. Yet – contrary to every expectation – a despised stranger ("a Samaritan") took a chance, and made himself vulnerable enough to take a look and give a hand. The hated enemy showed members of God's family how to have a human heart.

The most stunning feature lies in Jesus' reversal of the issue at stake in identifying one's neighbour – not the who deserves one's attention and care. Rather, Jesus challenges his listeners to become the kind of person who can "be a neighbour". Being a neighbour means showing compassion to everyone encountered – however frightening, alien, defenceless or naked that one might be. Jesus invites his hearers to risk life and possessions, as the Good Samaritan did.

The extraordinary wisdom of Jesus' teaching opens us to Paul's declarations about Christ in the epistle to the Colossians. Colossae was a small city in the Lycus River Valley in Phrygia (the southwestern section of modern Turkey). This small church seemingly struggled with current pseudo-philosophies, showing exaggerated interest in ascetical practices and a preoccupation with angelology.

Paul urged them to look to the Lord as the source of all their wisdom, since all else exists "through him and for him". Indeed, he declared, "in Christ all the fullness of God was pleased to dwell".

Sixteenth Sunday in Ordinary Time

Choosing the One Thing Needed, the Better Part

* Genesis 18.1-10a
* Psalm 15
* Colossians 1.24-28
* Luke 10.38-42

Pope Gregory the Great read in the story of Jesus' visit to the home of Martha and Mary the superiority of the contemplative life over the active one. Other interpreters have seen Martha and Mary representing, respectively, the present world and the world to come, Judaism and Christianity, justification by works and justification by faith. At its core, the story is a tiny jewel, exquisitely told by Luke, to help disciples sort out priorities in their lives.

Recent commentators, who tend to focus on the narrative links Luke has made in the overall structure of his work, stress the connections between this story and the parable of the Good Samaritan, which precedes it.

Just as that parable began with "a man", this tale begins with "a woman". The parable emphasized love of neighbour as it tried answer the question "Who is my neighbour?" This story implicitly takes up the question of love of God, which we might phrase in words such as the following: How and where may I manifest love of God?

In the Good Samaritan parable, Jesus helped clarify the person-to-person aspect of God's demand that disciples love others. Now the disciples' attention is turned to the vertical dimension of loving God, which Luke expresses as a preoccupation with the word of God brought by Jesus (Mary "sat at the Lord's feet and listened to what he was saying").

The parable, then, joined with the dialogue between Martha and Jesus, links the dimensions of loving God and loving one's neighbour so that, together, they make up the one great commandment of the law.

We learn from the story of Martha and Mary that the person who loves God must be taken up with God's word. Disciples discover this by listening to Jesus, as Mary did. Even when a person is apparently given over to serving within the kingdom – as Martha was – the practicalities of life can seduce one away from total attention to the things of God ("Martha, Martha, you are worried and distracted by many things").

Jesus gently reproached Martha before setting her straight. There is a difficulty with his message, because the manuscript traditions differ on what Jesus said. Some manuscripts read, "Few things are necessary, [or] only one", while other manuscripts read (as in our NRSV translation), "there is need of only one thing".

In any case, what constitutes the "one" thing or "few" things needed? Some interpreters think Jesus is preaching simplicity of life. Others think the issue has to do with hospitality. Only one or a few dishes are needed for a simple meal, but also attention must be given to the guest.

In this view, Mary has chosen to attend to the guest by conversation, while leaving her sister to do everything needing to be done in the kitchen. Faced with these two choices, Mary has claimed for herself the better task ("Mary has chosen the better part").

More likely, however, the meal context has simply been employed to illustrate a spiritual truth. Life in the world causes disciples to be stressed and fragmented. Attending to the word of God, however, gives one an integrating power that makes a singleness of vision possible.

It is important that attention to the cares of this world – even in service to God's kingdom – do not distract from the central need disciples have. They need to hear the word of God by listening in prayer at the feet of the Lord Jesus ("Mary has chosen the better part, which will not be taken away from her").

The story of Abraham playing host to God in the guise of three mysterious strangers is a story rich in subtle details that exemplifies Hebrew narrative style at its best.

Abraham's dozing is contrasted with the purposefully journeying men. Then, Abraham's frantic preparations are followed by the commanding silence of the men and their probing questions about Sarah. God, in the person of one of the travellers, promised to return "in due season" when elderly, barren Sarah would be blessed with a son.

Paul's contemplation revealed what underlies Christian existence in this world: "the riches of the glory of this mystery, which is Christ in you, the hope of glory".

Seventeenth Sunday in Ordinary Time

"Lord, Teach Us to Pray"

* Genesis 18.20-32
* Psalm 138
* Colossians 2.12-14
* Luke 11.1-13

In the reading from Genesis, the example of Abraham's intimate dialogue with God establishes that God, as judge of all the world, acts justly. In effect, Abraham negotiated with the Lord to the point that God was ready to avert the destruction of Sodom even if only ten righteous persons were found there. Abraham's example is meant to offer people confidence in approaching God, the heavenly Father, in prayer.

Just before this episode (Genesis 18.16-19), God had carried on a soliloquy, wondering aloud whether to share his plans with Abraham or not. For, in the ancient Near Eastern world, the servant of a god or king was privy to his master's plans. The Lord God concluded that, since Abraham's people would become great among the nations of the earth, it was only fitting that he learn that God does what is right by punishing only sinners.

Once God had announced the plan, Abraham began to dialogue. Abraham boldly asked God, "Will you indeed sweep away the righteous with the wicked?" After moving down from 50, through 45, 40, 30 and 20 righteous people needed to avert disaster for sinful Sodom, Abraham reached the natural limit of ten righteous ones. To all of the numbers of righteous people who would prevent the destruction of Sodom, God was agreeable.

Abraham had no need to descend below the natural threshold of ten righteous. For in the case of a number of righteous people below the limit of ten, God would reach out and save the individual righteous persons of Sodom, as proved to be the case with Lot and his family. At the close of the discussion, with God revealed as truly just, the dialogue ended, and Abraham and God departed.

From the reading from Colossians, disciples learn about not only God's justice but also his compassion, forgiving Jews and Greeks alike to create a wholly new righteous people, members of the Body of Christ, the Church. This happens for Christians through faith, in a sacramental rite, "when you were buried with Christ in baptism".

In the Apostle Paul's vision, the Father of Our Lord Jesus Christ "forgave us all our trespasses, erasing the record that stood against us with its legal demands". Paul concluded his powerful declaration of what God had done in redeeming sinners by Christ's death on the Cross, graphically stating that God set aside the reckoned sum of humanity's sins by "nailing it to the Cross".

Jesus includes the forgiveness of sins as one of several petitions to God that his disciples are to say "when[ever] you pray" ("And forgive us our sins, for we ourselves forgive everyone indebted to us"). The daily flow of divine forgiveness would be interrupted if, on the human level, there were not a corresponding practice of forgiveness.

The Lord's Prayer appears in the gospel tradition in two versions: a longer Matthean one (6.9-13) and the shorter version found in Luke. The example of Jesus' prayer in Gethsemane and on the Cross, his designation of God as "Abba" ("dear Father"), his various teachings on prayer, and the Lord's Prayer itself have exercised a tremendous impact on Christian devotion through the ages.

Variations of some of the petitions in the Lord's Prayer are found in the Gospels of Mark (11.25) and John (12.27). An early liturgical conclusion ("for yours is the kingdom and the power and the glory forever. Amen") has found its way into several Greek manuscripts of Matthew 6.13 and continues to be used in the liturgy of the Mass today.

The first petitions wish that God's name be sanctified, expressing a longing that the honour shown God in this world grow in extent, especially through the coming of God's kingdom. The petition for "daily bread" covers all that a person would need for subsistence, even though the meaning of the word translated as "daily" (*epiousios*) is not known elsewhere in Greek literature. Other suggested meanings include "spiritual", "supersubstantial", "essential" and "for the coming day".

Much has been written about the Lord's Prayer as the ideal, even perfect, prayer. It is characterized by familiarity with God as Father and its confident trust that God desires to answer the prayers of his children as loving parents long to respond to their children's requests (points that are also made in the parables that follow).

Eighteenth Sunday in Ordinary Time

"Vanity of Vanities! All Is Vanity"

* Ecclesiastes 1.2; 2.21-23
* Psalm 90

* Colossians 3.1-5, 9-11
* Luke 12.13-21

Though not numerous, among Jewish and Christian readers there have always been fans of this original thinker, named Ecclesiastes in Greek or Qoheleth in Hebrew ('the Preacher' in either case): skeptics, individuals with a dark vision of reality, and recovering alcoholics or those who follow other twelve-step programs.

Other readers of this book recall only a few of its epigrams ("What has been is what will be ... there is nothing new under the sun" [1.9] or "There is nothing better for mortals than to eat and drink, and find enjoyment in their toil" [2.24]) or its lyrical passages ("For everything there is a season, and a time for every matter under heaven: a time to be born, and a time to die; ... a time to weep and a time to laugh; ... a time to love and a time to hate; a time for war and a time for peace" [3.1-2, 4, 8]).

A learned commentator has summarized the key ideas of this wisdom writing as follows: human achievement is weak and impermanent; the fate of human beings is uncertain; human beings find it impossible to attain true knowledge and insight into the world; the goal of human striving needs to be joy, the divine imperative. Only the last boldly affirms life. But it points to something deep within human nature, an ineradicable desire for happiness planted by God. Living a moral life by following God's will, then, is the true pursuit of happiness.

In Hebrew, the doubling of a word makes it into a superlative. Thus 'the holy of holies' is the holiest place. And the absurdity of absurdities or "vanity of vanities" means the most absurd or most fleeting of realities. Yet this is how the Preacher characterizes life itself! It is exemplified by someone working hard to amass goods and property, only to have to leave them in death to someone who did not toil at all. For many in the world, life is sheer drudgery and pain ("even at night their mind does not rest").

What the sacred author wants people to realize is that life is absurd until meaning is thrust upon it by acts of courage and faith. The book stresses that God intends people to enjoy life. From clinging to that teaching there comes respite and relief from the sense of futility that people might otherwise experience.

Amid a collection of sayings on a wide variety of topics (Luke 12.1-59), Jesus warned against the belief that life consists in material goods ("Take care! Be on your guard against all kinds of greed; for one's life does not consist in the abundance of possessions"). Though he had been asked to mediate a family dispute about an inheritance, Jesus refused, hinting that avarice lay at the root of the conflict.

Then Jesus told a parable to reinforce his teaching. An already prosperous man began to make plans for the future out of a desire for security to enjoy to the full what he had acquired. He was heedless of the ultimate crisis for which he should have been ready: his death. God, the author of this crisis, called him a fool.

In his soliloquy, the rich man realized that the harvest's bounty had exceeded his expectations. His problem consisted in his desire to store it up for his use. The thought of sharing his abundance with people in need never crossed his mind. The man had shut everyone else out of his life and thoughts. There was no one else in the story until God called him to account.

The truism that life is threatened by death or the commonplace that "you can't take it with you when you die" receives an added dimension within the teaching of Jesus. In his preaching of the coming of God's kingdom, there lies a challenge that disciples not "store up treasures for themselves" but, instead, become "rich toward God". Jesus pleaded for a right evaluation and use of material wealth. Being truly "rich toward God" involved making use of one's riches, in obedience to God, to help the poor.

Paul noted that God had lavishly blessed sinners by raising them to newness of life with Christ. Their response must be a total self-renewal, including putting to death all self-seeking, "evil desire, and greed, which is idolatry".

Nineteenth Sunday in Ordinary Time

"Do Not Be Afraid, Little Flock"

* Wisdom 18.6-9
* Psalm 33
* Hebrews 11.1-2, 8-19
* Luke 12.32-48

Besides teachings on cross-bearing and obedience to the Father's will, Jesus taught about God's provident care for his children, on not being anxious for the future ("can any of you by worrying add a single hour to your span of life?" [Luke 12.25]).

Jesus referred to the trusting disposition that God's children are to have. They are to "Consider the ravens: they neither sow nor reap, they have neither storehouse nor barn, and yet God feeds them. Of how much more value are you than the birds!" (12.24).

What holds true for food applies also to clothing and other necessities of life ("Consider the lilies, how they grow: they neither toil nor spin; yet I tell you, even Solomon in all his glory was not clothed like one of these" [12.27]).

This does not mean believers are to sit around idly, but rather that trust in God leads to a proportionate response to the challenges of life in this world ("your Father knows that you need them ... strive for his kingdom, and all these things will be given to you as well" [12.30-31]). Unlike worldly folk, who are consumed with the pursuit of food and clothing, disciples are to seek first a relationship with God, knowing God's will and giving evidence of his purpose in their lives.

One of the weaknesses of the present lectionary readings is the omission of this important part of the teaching of Jesus on God's providence. The sayings in which Jesus invites his hearers to contemplate the way the heavenly Father cares for the birds of the air and the flowers of the fields appear twice in the gospel tradition (in Matthew 6.25-34 and Luke 12.22-32).

However, those who arranged the three-year cycle of readings chose to include only the Matthean version, which appears on the Eighth Sunday of Year A. As things work out, this gospel passage is almost invariably displaced by a Lenten Sunday, as in 2013 and 2016. In Year C, disciples hear from the lectionary only the closing words of Jesus as he urges that they be unafraid, "for it is your Father's good pleasure to give you the kingdom".

Jesus concluded his exhortation by addressing the disciples as a "little flock". The imagery suggests easily frightened sheep that need a shepherd's care. This, he assures them, is what God offers — everything associated with the kingdom for his sheep.

If disciples can begin to believe that God will provide generously, they, in turn, can be detached and generous in sharing their resources with others ("Sell your possessions and give alms ... Make ... for yourselves ... an unfailing treasure in heaven, where no thief comes near and no moth destroys").

The Book of Wisdom referred to the great night of the Exodus as the time when God called the Israelites to be a special possession from among all the nations of the earth ("you called us to yourself and glorified us"). This, too, was an instance of God's provident care for little ones, people of no consequence.

Jesus used the image of the Israelites' readiness on the night of their deliverance to describe the stance his disciples were to maintain constantly. Tying one's garments up around the waist was a picture of constant readiness for service (the words translated as "be dressed for action" interpret a text that literally means "let your loins be girded").

Disciples are to be ever at the alert, ready to serve one another, until Jesus' return at the end of time ("for the Son of Man is coming at an unexpected hour").

Since weddings in Jesus' day could last as long as a week, the master's return was not easily predictable. Servants had to be ready to serve him whenever he slipped away from the feasting. Those found at their tasks on his return would be blessed by the master and rewarded.

Jesus even suggested that the tables would be turned and disciples would find themselves being served by their Lord ("he will fasten his belt and have them sit down to eat, and he will come and serve them").

This rich image suggests total acceptance by Jesus. Representations of negligent servants slacking off are meant to startle such disciples into turning back towards a state of full-time alert and readiness for service.

Twentieth Sunday in Ordinary Time

Jesus' Journey into Fire and Baptism

* Jeremiah 38.4-6, 8-10
* Psalm 40
* Hebrews 12.1-4
* Luke 12.49-53

During the holiday period, North Americans drive long distances. On the highway they discover others who share the road: there are buses, trailers and campers, and every manner of truck. Long-distance rigs engender awe and respect. Here are skilled and experienced drivers doing a difficult job; one passes them only when there is lots of room and after checking twice to see that the way is clear. This is especially so when tailgate warnings warn of "Danger: Explosives" or "Highly Flammable Cargo".

Jesus' word that he has come to cast fire on the earth may stir in his followers thoughts of keeping their distance from him. For these are not the sentiments disciples typically associate with Jesus; indeed, the verse about Jesus casting fire on the earth is unique to Luke's Gospel.

In being baptized by John the Baptist, Jesus placed himself in solidarity with sinful humanity. Since Jesus had already undergone

John's baptism in water, a sign of repentance, the baptism Jesus alludes to must stand for his Passion. Mark hinted at the correctness of this observation when he linked Jesus' cup and his baptism (Mark 10.38-39).

Jesus' sayings present symbolic representations of a deep mystery, whose completion Luke probably understood to have taken place at Pentecost (cf. "tongues of fire" in Acts 2.3). Jesus both wished that a fire were ablaze in his disciples on earth and was anguished until his Passion would be complete. Like other mortals, Jesus recoiled before death, but unlike them, he was utterly devoted to the Father's will, which he had made his own.

Jesus' teaching describes the individual Christian's baptism into a fire able to purify believers from sin. His mystical language boldly proclaimed spiritual dimensions of the believer's baptism into Jesus' Paschal Mystery.

Jesus came as a messenger of peace (cf. Luke 2.14; 19.38). But saying that he came to bring not peace but division indicates that his peace is not a limp inheritance but a costly legacy. As Jesus was not spared testing, neither can the disciple be spared radical decision making. So, Jesus' word of division (Matthew 10.34 depicts Jesus bringing a sword) passes through society without sparing even disciples' families. Micah 7.6 predicted such divisions among families in the messianic age. Luke 21.16 says this was the experience of the early Church.

The Church saw in Jeremiah's personal difficult straits hints of the kind of rejection and suffering Jesus would endure. In 588–587 BC, King Zedekiah of Jerusalem visited cruel punishments on Jeremiah because he had foretold the city's impending destruction. An Ethiopian court advisor, Ebed-melech, pleaded on Jeremiah's behalf and won from the king a lessening of the harsh treatment meted out to the prophet. God informed Jeremiah that trust in God had motivated Ebed-melech's kindnesses (cf. Jeremiah 39.15-18).

Despite doing all he could to save his skin, Zedekiah came to death by not trusting in God's word. Jeremiah, by surrendering his life and cause into God's hands, survived the siege of Jerusalem safe and sound. This echoes the gospel paradox: "those who want to save their life will lose it; and those who lose their life for my sake ... will save it" (Mark 8.35).

For the early Christians, Jeremiah's rescue from the miry clay anticipated Jesus' resurrection. The psalmist recounts a similar experience in the responsorial psalm (Psalm 40).

In its literary structure, Hebrews is less an epistle than an exhortation to steadfastness in Christian faith. This is especially the case in the closing peroration of chapters 12 and 13. Christian life is depicted there as a race, with Jesus leading the pack of runners. He has already entered the glory reserved for the victors. The saints, too, particularly the heroes cited from the Old Testament, surround the Christian assembly, as it were cheering the runners on to finish the marathon.

One obstacle to victory is the "sin that clings so closely". Interpretations of this range from the sin of those who persecute Christians to pride and the weakness of Christians not yet fully free of sinful inclinations. An attractive interpretation sees this particular sin as yielding to despondency, thinking that the battle or race demands of Christians more than they can give. This finds support in the author's many references to perseverance as the antidote to sin. Perhaps, too, this is why Jesus is said to have disregarded the shame of the Cross "for the sake of the joy that was set before him".

As the "pioneer and perfecter of our faith", Jesus leads Christians and brings them to fullness of faith. In gratitude, Christians are urged to be faithful unto death as Jesus was.

Twenty-first Sunday in Ordinary Time

"Lord, Will Only a Few Be Saved?"

* Isaiah 66.18-21
* Psalm 117
* Hebrews 12.5-7, 11-13
* Luke 13.22-30

Once, while crossing the university campus where I worked, I was approached by a young person who asked whether I had been saved. "Yes, I believe I have," I replied, then hurried on. As I walked away, I thought of the many nuances I would need to add to explain what was involved in saying 'yes'.

Many have had the same issue put to them at their doorstep or at the mall by evangelists who ask such questions as "Have you accepted Jesus as your personal Lord and Saviour?" Periodically, preachers come on the scene and stir up in people concerns about the end of the world and about who or how many will be saved.

In other words, things have not changed much since the time of Jesus. When people had been suggesting that perhaps nothing much would become of his movement of renewal in Israel, Jesus told two parables of God's kingdom (Luke 13.18-22).

Though a mustard seed is the smallest, it soon becomes a large bush in which birds may nest. Once a tiny bit of leaven is mixed in with three measures of flour, it soon leavens the whole batter.

Discerning his message, someone asked Jesus, "Lord, will only a few be saved?" Typically, Jesus' answer was parabolic. The door is narrow. The owner of the house will refuse entry to many who presumed they had been invited. Still others, from a long way off, however, will gain admission.

Faced with these facts, what is a disciple of Jesus to do? "Strive to enter through the narrow door". Jesus invited his hearers to "strive", a word used of athletes as they discipline themselves to win a competition. Though the kingdom is God's gift, people must vigorously engage themselves in the process of their own salvation.

Paul summarized the paradoxical nature of salvation when he urged the Philippians to "work out your own salvation with fear and trembling, for it is God who is at work in you, enabling you both to will and to work for his good pleasure" (2.12-13).

Jesus engages his hearers by inviting them to imagine themselves outside a shut door: "you begin to stand outside and to knock at the door, saying 'Lord, open to us'". All of a sudden, the disguise is dropped and Jesus is revealed as the householder. He will say to the

Galileans and Judeans of the first century, "I do not know where you come from ... go away from me, all you evildoers!"

People will claim association with Jesus: "We ate and drank with you, and you taught in our streets". True companionship with Jesus, however, involves living by faith in God. So Jesus asked people to imagine themselves cast out where "there will be weeping and gnashing of teeth" so that they might have a change of heart, accept his message and enter the end-time kingdom.

When the kingdom comes fully, many in Israel or the Church, who presumed themselves included, will be surprised to find themselves outside. By contrast, Gentiles, the poor and outcast – whom others might have thought excluded – "will come from east and west, from north and south, and will eat in the kingdom of God".

In reply to the question "Lord, will only a few be saved?" Jesus effectively answered, "No". But his reply also challenges each person with a counter-question: "Will the saved include you?"

God's saving design for the whole world, proclaimed by Jesus, was beautifully foretold in the closing words of the Book of Isaiah. God's purpose is to take people from every nation, commissioning them for priestly service to the divine praise and glory.

The challenge in following Jesus was combined with a message of encouragement in the Epistle to the Hebrews. The author argued that God's discipline, which comes upon Christians as they follow Jesus' way, may seem painful at times. But each should realize that such trials are like the discipline that a parent gives a child, and are signs of love and acceptance.

Finally, divine discipline yields an abundant harvest of righteousness. Therefore, Christians are exhorted to lift up their drooping hands and strengthen their weak knees "so that what is lame may not be put out of joint, but rather be healed".

Twenty-second Sunday in Ordinary Time

"Those Who Humble Themselves Will Be Exalted"

* Sirach 3.17-20, 28-29
* Psalm 68
* Hebrews 12.18-19, 22-24a
* Luke 14.1, 7-14

Around the year 180 BC, Jesus the son of Sirach gave instruction on wisdom to the youth of Jerusalem. His counsels and maxims told how one could become a success in life, how one could please God and other people.

Modesty and humility were part of the ideal towards which the would-be wise person aspired. For these virtues were a reflection of Israel's God, who had chosen to be close to the poor and needy, as the Psalm today tells us: "Father of orphans and protector of widows is God in his holy habitation. God gives the desolate a home to live in; he leads out the prisoners to prosperity".

Sirach pointed out that the humble person "will be loved by those whom God accepts". Within God's household, then, all should come to share a single outlook. Sirach's principle was that "The greater you are, the more you must humble yourself; so you will find favour in the sight of the Lord".

Gospel humility is not the fawning humility of a Uriah Heep in Dickens' *David Copperfield*. Rather, true humility is that which acknowledges one's primary status as that of a creature of God. Each person is made in the divine likeness and constantly receives all good things from God: life, abilities, achievements, all that one has come to have and possess: "to the humble the Lord reveals his secrets".

Therefore, no one claims talents or endowments – or the achievements that these allow one to accomplish – as anything other than divinely bestowed gifts, to be used for God's glory. The honour or status that a person receives through recognition by others is put into true perspective only when one realizes that the only true standing is that which one has in the eyes of God.

In the ancient world, meals were important social ceremonies where little was left to chance. In Luke's Gospel, we find observations that people noted where and with whom one ate (5.29-30), whether one performed hand-washing rituals before meals (11.38), and where one sat to eat.

Pliny the Younger's *Letters* critiqued the meal etiquette of his day, noting that the amount and quality of food depended on how close one sat to the host: "some very elegant dishes were served up to himself and a few more of the company; while those which were placed before the rest were cheap and paltry".

Jesus exposed the grasping dispositions that motivated both host and guests. Though some think he simply counselled guests how to play the game more shrewdly ("so that when your host comes, he may say to you, 'Friend, move up higher'"), Jesus did not suggest the guest take a place several notches below his or her station. Instead, Jesus advised his disciples to take the "lowest place".

The "honour" or glory each would receive resided as much in God's presence as in their standing among mortals whose perspective was limited. Jesus hints at the end-time reward of heaven: "for whoever exalts himself will be humbled, and whoever humbles himself will be exalted [by God]".

Likewise, Jesus' advice to hosts is directed at God's end-time rewards. Hosts are prone to being hooked by the reciprocity system, thinking that 'those I invite must invite me in return; I will benefit not only from good meals but also from the honour and status associated with the wealthy and powerful'.

Gospel values require that one *not* invite "your friends or your brothers or sisters or your relatives or rich neighbours", but rather "the poor, the crippled, the lame, and the blind". Because these cannot repay you now, their patron – God! – will repay you at the "resurrection of the righteous".

Following the advice of Jesus means entering into a new value system where God does the rewarding and continues giving generously.

God's abundant giving also underlies the passage from Hebrews. There the Christian assembly is invited to see itself joining God's festal gathering, where all share the status of "the firstborn who are enrolled in heaven" and "the spirits of the righteous made perfect" by the "new covenant" God established through Jesus.

This is not a frightening reality – as one might imagine the encounter at Mount Sinai was – but implies being part of an assembly permeated by joy and peace.

Twenty-third Sunday in Ordinary Time

Facing the Christian's Dilemma with Philemon

* Wisdom 9.13-18
* Psalm 90
* Philemon 9b-10, 12-17
* Luke 14.25-33

At 25 verses, Paul's epistle to Philemon is among the shortest of New Testament writings. And its theme, the treatment of Philemon's runaway slave Onesimus, might appear to have no relevance today.

But its subtle handling of the demands of brotherhood – insofar as they surpass the requirements of justice – speaks to every era, including ours. Paul also observed that, though he could command Philemon to do the right thing, he would much rather allow the Spirit to lead Philemon to choose the loving way.

Philemon, a wealthy Christian, had experienced the loss of a valuable asset when Onesimus fled his household after defrauding him. Having come to know Paul, Onesimus sought asylum with him in prison and there became a Christian ("whose father I have become during my imprisonment").

According to Roman law, fugitive slaves had to be returned to their masters; anyone harbouring a fugitive slave was subject to a fine. Paul sent Onesimus back to Philemon bearing this letter. He asked Philemon to accept him "no longer as a slave but more than a slave, a beloved brother".

In his rhetorical appeal, Paul made a pun on Onesimus' name, which means "useful" ("formerly he was *useless* to you, but now he is indeed *useful* both to you and to me" [v. 11]).

Receiving Onesimus as a brother implied that Philemon had forgiven Onesimus a debt at Paul's request. This led Paul to muse aloud to Philemon about how much he owed Paul for the gift of faith! Lastly, though ostensibly written to Philemon, the letter was addressed also to Apphia (likely Philemon's wife) and the congregation that met in their house. Did Paul consciously put Philemon on the spot – challenging him to be generous – by asking that the letter be read in the house church assembly?

Philemon's dilemma pitted his rights (what was owed to him in justice) against letting himself be led by love's demands. Though Paul did not recommend the abolition of slavery (a major social institution of his time), he urged his fellow Christian not to treat a slave as property but as a human person. Paul also left him free to make his own decision in love.

We do not know how Philemon handled the dilemma presented to him by Paul. But an early tradition tells of a bishop named Onesimus, which may account for the preservation of this brief Pauline letter.

The gospel suggests that Paul learned to set dilemmas before Christian disciples from Jesus himself. For surrendering to the demands of the kingdom means viewing Jesus as the only teacher. And Jesus will not let those who want to follow him squirm their way out of the implications of his teaching. Nothing must get in the way of following Jesus, not even family ties, if they take one away from his way.

In the sentence "Whoever comes to me and does not hate their father and mother ... and even their life itself", the word "hate" is being used figuratively. It refers to a priority relationship, as we can see from the parallel version in Matthew's Gospel: "Whoever loves father or mother more than me is not worthy of me" (10.37). Jesus and the kingdom are the priority relationship; all else comes after.

To illustrate, Jesus tells two stories about a person building a watchtower and about a king going to war. Each must calculate the cost in resources, whether the initiative is totally one's own (building the tower) or is forced from outside (a king discovers that he is outnumbered two to one). Entering into these exercises leaves the disciple realizing that he or she must reflect on what it will take to finish the project of being Jesus' disciple: not less than everything! "So therefore, whoever of you does not give up all their possessions cannot be my disciple".

How inscrutable is this wisdom taught by Paul and Jesus in dilemmas and parables! And this is precisely the point put in a variety of ways by the Book of Wisdom: "For who can learn the counsel of God?"

But divine wisdom that is helpful for living life well in this world is given by God's Holy Spirit: "people were taught what pleases you, and were saved by wisdom".

Twenty-fourth Sunday in Ordinary Time

The Joy of Being Found

* Exodus 32.7-11, 13-14
* Psalm 51
* 1 Timothy 1.12-17
* Luke 15.1-32

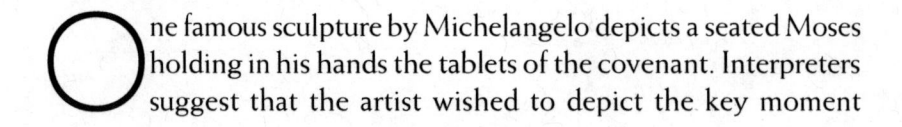

One famous sculpture by Michelangelo depicts a seated Moses holding in his hands the tablets of the covenant. Interpreters suggest that the artist wished to depict the key moment when Moses discovered the rebellion of God's people (the golden calf episode) but was not yet certain what to do. White-hot anger and deep wells of compassion mingled in his breast, and it was not yet clear which response would predominate.

Today's reading from Exodus boldly suggests that such a struggle was also waging in God's heart. Attributing human emotions to God, the sacred author tried to suggest that the behaviour of the chosen people merited their obliteration. It was as if God wanted to start over, beginning again with Moses ("of you I will make a great nation"). Moses learned compassion from his encounters with God and, after Moses and God consulted together, the earlier plan went forward.

That human compassion can help people understand the depths of God's affection and care for lost sinners is the message of the parable of the Prodigal Son and his brother. Some have suggested that the parable might be better entitled "the Prodigal Father", for he lavishly wanted to pour out riches and compassion on both his sons.

In trying to understand the parable of the father and his sons, it is important to realize how Jesus' audience would have thought about the father's behaviour towards his sons. In the Mediterranean culture of the time, the father disregarded a pivotal value of his era: his honour. By his solicitude for his sons and his attempts to win them to reconciliation and joy, he shamed himself in the eyes of those who heard Jesus speak the parable.

If we are meant to take the father of the parable as an example of how God acts in favour of the sinner, we must conclude that God's action is surprising. God even risks the shame of going beyond expected human categories in order to draw his sons and daughters into the fullness of divine family life. All of this was so that they might know of the new life being offered to those on the verge of perishing.

Underlying the whole parable's message is the notion of joy at being found. This links the parable of the father and his boys with the two earlier parables of the lost sheep and lost silver coin. The shepherd who found his sheep and the woman who found her silver coin – after diligent searching – shared their joy with friends and neighbours. These social expressions of joy model the joy found in heaven on the conversion of sinners ("there is joy in the presence of the Angels of God over one sinner who repents").

The parable of the shepherd looking for his lost sheep (the basis of Jesus' own mission) added a provocative comparison. For Jesus said, "there will be more joy in heaven over one sinner who repents than over ninety-nine righteous persons who need no repentance". This does not at all mean that God has no interest in the righteous. Only that God wants *all* to share life in the kingdom. When a sinner returns to God, heaven feels a party is in order. In fact, this hoped-for joy in the conversion of sinners kept Jesus interacting with sinners.

We are not given any psychological insight into the sinner's joy in being found. But all the external manifestations of the son's acceptance by his father (robe, ring, sandals and the family celebration with fatted calf and music) suggest a joy that permeated his whole appearance, status and being.

The dignity that the father put off, his son puts on. The only unanswered question at the end is whether the elder son would share in the joy of his brother's homecoming. It is a question the hearers of the parable might ask themselves: Would I join in the feasting if I were in his place?

The second reading, from First Timothy, describes the joy of the Apostle Paul at being found by Christ Jesus on the road to Damascus. Boldly he could say, "Christ Jesus came into the world to save sinners" and that, in his own eyes, "I am the foremost".

Twenty-fifth Sunday in Ordinary Time

Learning Decisiveness from a Crafty Steward

* Amos 8.4-7
* Psalm 113

* 1 Timothy 2.1-7
* Luke 16.1-13

In recent years, with the global economy in crisis and various currencies being devalued, the economy has been on everyone's mind. Though based on a very different view of money and its hold on people's lives, the scriptural texts this Sunday and next offer lessons on a proper perspective on money.

Wealth in the Bible and in the Church's teaching is a blessing from God. For one's ability to labour and to earn money – let us say, even an ability to make use of market forces to develop capital – is a gift from God.

In biblical perspective, money has definite purposes, among which are meeting the needs of the poor along with sustaining one's own health and meeting one's responsibilities to others (cf. 2 Corinthians 9.8-10). Sharing one's possessions stands out as a demand of the kingdom of God, which confronts individuals in the preaching of Jesus (cf. Luke 3.11).

In late biblical times – at the dawn of the New Testament era – wealth came to be viewed somewhat negatively, because God-fearing people saw massive poverty existing alongside great wealth. It was but a short step to conclude that the riches of the very few had been acquired, in some sense, at the expense of the numerous poor.

When judgments were made on life in a given society, the wealthy sometimes became the object of a prophet's reproach or attack (cf. Amos). This was especially so when those with an abundance of goods were lacking in compassion for the needy. In Jesus' instruction, a frequent theme was the great difficulty of salvation for the rich, unless their lives were marked by repentance (cf. Luke 18.27; 19.1-10).

In a period of prosperity, the prophet Amos denounced those who thought only of buying and selling ("buying [as slaves] the poor for silver and the needy for a pair of sandals, and selling the sweepings of the wheat").

Amos argued that the desire for money had blinded his fellow Israelites. Forgetting to take God into the equation led them to eliminate others from their consciences. God's commandment "You shall not steal" undergirds truly just relations, both interpersonal and social.

In chapter 16, Luke gathered together a collection of sayings by Jesus about the potential as well as the danger inherent in riches. Today's parable of the unjust or crafty steward, whom Jesus praised, has unsettled Christians since the earliest days of the faith. For in it Jesus complimented a corrupt steward for his resourcefulness once his misconduct had been found out.

A steward was expected to be a person of integrity, but the corruption of the protagonist of Jesus' story had been found out, and he faced dismissal. Handing the accounts over to his master, however, would take time; the steward seized on this window of opportunity to secure his future.

Possessed of a great deal of latitude to write and rewrite contracts for his master, the steward used the little time he had left to show generosity to his master's debtors, thereby placing them in a debt of gratitude to himself.

In the ancient world, the reciprocity ethic held sway. Good turns given called for future benefits in return. Public honour would require that the debtors offer benefits to the steward in the future. Thus, he had secured his future. Could Jesus' disciples similarly meet the challenge of the kingdom's arrival in their midst with the same despatch?

Jesus did not condone wrongdoing by the steward, but rather praised the agility and speed with which the steward sized up the situation and took action at a time of personal crisis. Jesus observed that the steward's ability to provide for his future is something that his disciples (the "children of light") could and should emulate when deciding how to respond to the crisis situation they were being placed in by the demands of his message.

Boldly Jesus urged, "Make friends for yourselves by means of dishonest wealth so that when it is gone, they may welcome you into the eternal homes".

In other sayings, Jesus expressed his own prophetic critique of wealth, noting that personified money ("Mammon" [Wealth]) – when sought as an end in itself – quickly becomes a tyrannical master, a veritable rival to God. "You cannot serve God and wealth!" (Matthew 6.24).

Twenty-sixth Sunday in Ordinary Time

Sharing Wealth with God's Poor

* Amos 6.1a, 4-7
* Psalm 146
* 1 Timothy 6.11-16
* Luke 16.19-31

Today's Old Testament reading and gospel present biting criticisms of luxurious living. Each faults those who possess an abundance of goods for their failure to show compassion. The psalm describes God as the champion of the dispossessed of every kind. Finally, the epistle calls to mind the commitment of the baptized to live their faith.

The prophet Amos denounced what today we would call conspicuous consumption. The seer's stinging criticism noted signs of opulence, people lying on "beds of ivory" and "lounging on their couches". He observed excess as they drank wine by the bowlful rather than from a goblet, in moderation.

Amos preached his message in the second quarter of the eighth century BC. It was a time of apparent peace that seemed to promise increasing prosperity. The northern kingdom dreamed of grandeurs to come.

Especially among the residents of Samaria – to whom the words we hear today were addressed – luxury and a certain snobbishness held sway. Beneath the superficial calm, however, a social cancer lay lurking.

Into this dream world Amos came preaching a social gospel rooted in radical faith in God alone. To those who lacked a social conscience, Amos promised the first place in the coming deportation.

Faithful Samaritans ought to have cared for the poor with whom they were bound in a common faith. Instead, they cared not at all for the "ruin of Joseph", their community of faith and culture. Their indifference would be met with a divinely imposed recompense.

The positive side of Amos' proclamation foreshadowed that of the gospel of Jesus. He inquired of his hearers what things they possessed that they had not received from God, wondering how they could boast of them as if they were their own (cf. 1 Corinthians 4.7).

By stressing God's identification with the lot of the poor, Amos anticipated what Jesus would say: "just as you did to one of the least of these who are members of my family, you did to me" (Matthew 25.40).

If the epistle reading had begun one verse earlier, it would have linked much better with the other readings of today's Mass. There, Paul noted, "the love of money is a root of all kinds of evil, and in their eagerness to be rich some have wandered away from the faith and pierced themselves with many pains" (1 Timothy 6.10).

Next, Christians hear an exhortation to the opposite course of action: "pursue righteousness, godliness, faith, love, endurance, gentleness". The stakes are high; the goal is eternal life.

In order to urge Timothy on, Paul recalled the moment of his profession. This may have been the time of his consecration to ministry, but more likely the phrase evokes Timothy's baptismal commitment. The Christian's commitment naturally summons up the great profession made by Jesus before the Roman procurator, Pontius Pilate (cf. John 18.36-37). Disciples are urged to imitate Jesus their Lord.

An aspect of the teaching of Jesus regularly emphasized in Luke's Gospel is the prudent use of material possessions. Throughout Luke's narrative of Jesus' journey to Jerusalem (Luke 9.51–19.27), he offered instruction to various groups. In this case, Jesus spoke to the Pharisees who were said to be "lovers of money" (16.14) and illustrated his saying that "what is prized by human beings is an abomination in the sight of God" (16.15).

Jesus' teaching in this parable, the only one in which a character is given a proper name (Lazarus), illustrates the "eternal homes" spoken of in the parable of the Dishonest Steward (16.9). Likewise, it emphasizes the reversal of situations taught earlier about the rich and poor (6.20, 24).

The parable has two parts: in the first, Jesus taught that in the afterlife there is a counterbalancing of the situation that held sway in this life; in the second, Jesus argued that even a messenger from the dead cannot effect repentance among rich people whose hearts have been hardened against the poor.

Adapting Jesus' message to our wealthy secularized world remains a very delicate task. Of primary importance is that the interpretation of preachers and teachers not induce false guilt among fellow Christians. Rather, they should help the message of Jesus to penetrate the hearts of those who have not yet heard his summons, namely to follow him in that true poverty of spirit to which he calls disciples.

Twenty-seventh Sunday in Ordinary Time

Living by Faith in God

* Habakkuk 1.2-3, 2.2-4
* Psalm 95
* 2 Timothy 1.6-8, 13-14
* Luke 17.5-10

Little is known about the prophet Habakkuk except what we may deduce from his oracles. His reference to the Chaldeans (1.6) makes it likely that he was active in the last quarter of the seventh century BC.

The Qumran community, which authored or collected the Dead Sea Scrolls, produced a commentary on Habakkuk, applying the prophet's message to their own situation.

Paul made use of part of a verse from Habakkuk ("the righteous live by their faith" [2.4a]) in Romans 1.17 and Galatians 3.11. These texts, in turn, were important to Martin Luther's Church Reformation project, highlighting – as they do – "justification by faith".

A short work of 56 verses, the message of Habakkuk differs from many prophetic works in that the oracles present a systematically developed argument. It begins with a lament over the rampant injustices of Judean society. God replies to the prophet's reproof by announcing that the Chaldeans will be his agents to rectify injustice.

Astonished by this news, Habakkuk boldly objects that God's solution is worse than the original problem! God answers this "complaint" by promising a vision, which the prophet is to wait for in confidence: "there is still a vision…; it speaks of the end, and does not lie. If it seems to tarry, wait for it; it will surely come, it will not delay". The basic principle underlying the vision is that, by contrast with people who are arrogant, those who are righteous base their lives on their steadfast faith.

Only in chapter 3 does God's promised vision come into focus. In this further revelation, Habakkuk depicts God as a divine warrior marching to the rescue of his people (3.3-15). Finally, Habakkuk confesses his willingness to wait with a trusting disposition for God to overcome the problem of injustice, which troubled him personally for a long time.

Jesus, too, spoke of living by faith in God. Luke's version of his saying on having "faith the size of a mustard seed" appears, with variations, also in Matthew 17.20 and 21.21. In one Matthean version, faith is able to cast a mountain into the sea. The formulation found in Luke, however, speaks of the tiniest measure of faith telling "this mulberry tree, 'Be uprooted and planted in the sea,' and it would obey you".

Jesus made this pronouncement when the disciples had asked him to "Increase our faith!" They assumed that they had faith – whether faith is conceived as a dynamic process one can grow in, or as something not just a matter of their own strength but something Jesus can add to.

Jesus' reply is surprising, implying they did not have even that degree of faith one could compare with the tiny mustard seed. For, if they did, they could order a sycamore (mulberry) tree to be "planted" in the sea – an odd idea, which indicates that the images may have become confused as Jesus' saying on faith was handed on. Even with the slightest bit of faith, Jesus' disciples should be able to live his teaching.

A parable about a slave serving without reward closes out this small gospel unit. Unfortunately, it seems to cast God in the unappealing image of a slave driver. Even Christians who are well schooled in the doctrine of justification by faith occasionally feel they deserve a reward for the goodness of their lives and deeds.

What the parable asserts, however, through Jesus' exhortation that, at the end of the day, disciples humbly say, "We are worthless slaves; we have done only what we ought to have done!" is that God's blessings and favours are ultimately matters only of grace. They cannot be earned.

Paul always stressed the supernatural origin of his vocation, and in today's epistle recalls his own role in Timothy's vocation "through the laying on of my hands". Through this commissioning, God gave – and gives – the Church's ordained ministers not a "spirit of cowardice, but rather a spirit of power and of love and of self-discipline".

The conferral of the Spirit is all God's doing. Still, the individual gospel minister is not passive. Rather, he can do as Timothy was enjoined, "to rekindle the gift of God that is within you". This, too, comes from God, for it is effected "with the help of the Holy Spirit living in us".

Twenty-eighth Sunday in Ordinary Time

A Samaritan Teaches Gratitude

* 2 Kings 5.14-17
* Psalm 98

* 2 Timothy 2.8-13
* Luke 17.11-19

Tracing their lineage to the old northern kingdom, Samaritans were reckoned by Jews to be neither Jews nor Gentiles. They were treated with suspicion, hostility. But such marginal types were the very people Jesus came to seek out and to save.

Outsiders, whether Samaritans or lepers, are the special focus of Jesus' ministry, possibly because they are open to seeing God at work in a way that ordinary believers are not. For, after his healing, Naaman recognized the special status of Israel's saving Lord and declared, "Now I know that there is no God in all the earth except in Israel".

More than the others, Luke's Gospel features Samaritans. At the outset of Jesus' journey, readers learn of a Samaritan village that refused to give him hospitality because "his face was set toward Jerusalem" (9.51-56).

Samaritans responded well to the preaching of the gospel (cf. Acts 1.8; 8.1-25) and became models of behaviour, as in the parable of the Good Samaritan, and in today's gospel, which introduces the grateful Samaritan, a leper who returned to give thanks to Jesus for cleansing him.

For those steeped in the Bible, the narrative of a leper's healing would naturally evoke memories of the leper cured by the prophet Elisha (2 Kings 5.1-27). Jesus cited Naaman's healing to the citizens of his hometown as justification for going beyond those who think they have claims on his ministry by kinship or personal acquaintance, to serve outsiders instead: "There were also many lepers in Israel in the time of Elisha, and none of them was cleansed except Naaman, the Syrian" (Luke 4.27).

The liturgical selection is a truncated account of Naaman's physical healing and subsequent coming to faith. It omits Naaman's initial reluctance to trust the word of Elisha's servant (2 Kings 5.9-13). It focuses, rather, on the healing itself, Naaman's profession of faith, Elisha's selflessness in refusing recompense, and the decision by the converted pagan Naaman to worship only the God of Israel.

Possessed of a rather simplistic faith, Naaman thought he could only adore the God of Israel on Israelite soil, and so begged two mule-loads of earth to take back to Syria, on which he would offer God burnt offerings and holocausts.

Biblical tradition struggles to explain the link between illnesses of the body and sins that afflict the soul. One must not be led to think that someone suffering from an illness – leprosy, for example – is being punished by God for the commission of one sin or another. Rather, sickness reflects the normal state of humanity, which is wounded and incomplete. Physical illnesses and moral disorders are the ordinary lot of mortals, human beings who are fragile and sinful.

This explains why all healings brought about through the invocation of God's name are signs of the divine purpose, which intends to put an end to the travails that weigh upon God's children. God does not want the death of sinners, but desires that they be converted and live (cf. Ezekiel 18.23). The healing granted to a particular person becomes, then, a pledge of the hope of salvation all people should entertain in their hearts.

Biblical accounts of healings usually feature ritual gestures that spell out this link with God's purpose. Such would underlie Jesus' instruction to the ten lepers: "Go and show yourselves to the priests". This command speaks of the healing of the soul that God desires and that is symbolized by physical healings. Along with physical restoration to health, one must envisage liturgies of pardon, celebratory rites of redemption granted.

The Naaman story reveals a double healing: the restoration of his flesh to be "like the flesh of a young boy" and the opening of his heart to discover the true God. So, too, does the story of the ten lepers. All receive physical healing, but nine are satisfied with staying on the physical level alone.

One, a Samaritan heretic, is shown to be touched by the grace of thanksgiving: gratitude. His faith has doubly saved him. He rendered thanks to God – as Christians do at the Eucharist – for healing that was both physical and spiritual.

Paul's gratitude to God extended even to the circumstances of his imprisonment for the gospel. Paul knew he might prove unfaithful, but not Christ: "he remains faithful – for he cannot deny himself".

Twenty-ninth Sunday in Ordinary Time

Jesus Urges Perseverance in Prayer

* Exodus 17.8-13
* Psalm 121
* 2 Timothy 3.14–4.2
* Luke 18.1-8

The fourth and last section of the *Catechism of the Catholic Church* is devoted to prayer in the life of the Christian disciple.

The initial part cites St. John Damascene's definition of prayer as "the raising of one's mind and heart to God or the requesting of good things from God".

Then, the Catechism mentions biblical types of prayer, such as "The prayer of Moses [that] responds to the living God's initiative for the salvation of his people. It foreshadows the prayer of intercession of the unique mediator, Christ Jesus" (#2593).

Moses' role as mediator of God's saving design is clearly shown in passages where he asks for God's compassion towards sinful Israel (such as in Exodus 32–34). By contrast, Moses' effectiveness as a man of God seems magical in the way he obtains victory for Israel in the war against Amalek ("Whenever Moses held up his hands, Israel prevailed; and whenever he lowered his hands, Amalek prevailed").

The desert tribe of Amalekites carried out raids against Israel in the wilderness and remained Israel's enemy even after their settlement in the Promised Land (cf. Judges 6; 1 Samuel chapters 15, 27, 30). Joshua, who appears in the biblical narrative for the first time in this passage and whose name means "The LORD [Yahweh] saves", became God's instrument, winning victory for Israel.

Though Joshua led the troops and Moses did not enter the fray, it is clear that the latter was the key figure in obtaining the victory. For this battle was no ordinary military incursion.

The narrative offers a twofold focus: on Joshua's leadership and on the staff in the hands of Moses, symbolic of God's power to save. Genuine human prowess and God's will become delicately intertwined in this saving moment.

St. Paul developed war imagery when describing the believer's struggle against Satan, sin and death. People also speak today about the war against poverty, cancer or illiteracy.

While one may wonder about the contribution of Moses' upraised hands at a distance from the battle to Israel's victory, the biblical witness invites faith from the disciple's heart.

Perhaps because our world focuses a great deal on secondary, mainly human, causes in interpreting what happens in the world, it is sometimes difficult for people to find room for God's role in ordinary life. Is it possible, then, to believe in God today? This is the question Jesus posed at the end of his parable about the need to pray without getting discouraged: "when the Son of Man comes, will he find faith on earth?"

The expectation that widows would be cared for was strong in Israel, for God would vindicate their cause. This outlook was carried over into the early Church: "Religion that is pure and undefiled before God, the Father, is this: to care for orphans and widows, and to keep oneself unstained by the world" (James 1.27).

But the judge in Jesus' parable was described as someone who "neither feared God nor had respect for any human being". In his soliloquy, the judge even made this description his own. What hope, then, did the poor widow have of obtaining justice – presumably deserved – in her grievance against a third party? The judge was her only recourse, and persistence appeared to be the only tactic available to her.

Interior monologues are favourite devices in the parables of Jesus handed on by Luke, as we have seen in recent weeks in the parables of the Rich Fool (12.17-19), the Prodigal Son (15.17-19) and the Crafty Steward (16.3-4). So we are not surprised at discovering the judge's reasoning this way.

The judge gave two reasons for reaching a decision to grant her petition: first, "because this widow keeps bothering me", and second, "so that she may not wear me out by continually coming". Generally today, the second reason gets translated metaphorically. However, its literal meaning may be rendered "so that in the end she may not come and strike me under the eye"! She might have given him a black eye physically or by ruining his reputation.

Jesus' parable teaches a double lesson. His disciples can learn from the widow to be persistent, earnest and never lose heart in prayer. And they can be reassured, as disciples, that God answers those who pray day and night, for, in the words of the Psalm, "Our help is from the Lord, who made heaven and earth".

Thirtieth Sunday in Ordinary Time

"God, Be Merciful to Me, a Sinner"

* Sirach 35.15-17, 20-22
* Psalm 34
* 2 Timothy 4.6-8, 16-18
* Luke 18.9-14

Earlier in the Gospel of Luke, Jesus had enunciated a general principle: "whoever exalts himself will be humbled, and whoever humbles himself will be exalted" (14.11). There it was the conclusion to Jesus' teaching on manners at banquets, as he urged people to take lower seats rather than those of honour. Now, this same axiom is shown to be a spiritual one, holding true even in God's house.

Jesus told a parable about two types of religious persons one might notice frequenting the Jerusalem Temple. They are at opposite ends of the spectrum as far as observance of the law is concerned.

One was zealous for the affairs of God. The other's occupation, as the agent of a hated occupying power, led him to be lumped in with "sinners", those on the verge of excommunication from the faith community.

The religiously motivated person ("a Pharisee") boasted of a piety that caused him to keep separate from others ("I thank you that I am not like other people: thieves, rogues, adulterers, or even like this tax collector").

This "righteous" person's prayer has echoes elsewhere in the Bible, where Israel thanked God for its election and privileges. His fasting practices were not merely the few obligatory public fasts, but a twice-weekly devotion that many Jews followed in their piety. Since he also tithed – not just on the grain, wine and oils as prescribed, but "a tenth of all my income" – the Pharisee manifested his devotion through almsgiving.

Thus, prayer, fasting and almsgiving – the pillars of biblical devotion – figured greatly among this Pharisee's values. Still, something was wrong. For Luke observed that Jesus told this parable "to some who trusted in themselves that they were righteous, and regarded others with contempt".

The good churchgoer's religion – if we may adapt the parable to Jesus' disciples in the church of every age – can become the means to personal self-aggrandizement instead of serving to nurture a sincere affect for the things of God.

For his part, the tax collector took no note of who else was near him during his prayer. Not daring even to lift his eyes heavenward, he beat his breast as a sign of repentance and humility and begged God's compassion ("God, be merciful to me, a sinner!"). "Standing far off", the sinful tax collector did not dare to approach where the righteous stood. His only reliance was on God's forgiveness.

Jesus observed how the tax collector's prayer was heard and the Pharisee's was not: "I tell you, this man went down to his home justified rather than the other". Jesus' word reveals the true state – before God, the source of justification – of human hearts, that may be quite different from what external appearances suggest.

In a similar vein, Ben Sira declared that, while showing no partiality, God does not ignore the lot of the lowly, such as the wronged, orphans and widows. Indeed, the prayer of the humble enjoys special power, as it "pierces the clouds, and it will not rest until it reaches its goal".

Paul used dramatic images to symbolize the nearness of his death. "I am already being poured out as a libation" is an allusion to the wine poured out upon ritual temple sacrifices.

"The time of my departure" evokes impressions of breaking camp or letting a ship loose from its moorings, both common euphemisms for death in antiquity.

Paul also expressed a serene sense of accomplishment, one deriving not from his strength alone but from something he had been enabled to achieve with Christ's power ("the Lord stood by me and gave me strength").

Two athletic images lead into a concluding religious summary of Paul's ministry: "I have fought the good fight, I have finished the race, I have kept the faith".

All that remained for Paul was to accept God's final gift, the culmination of a life of blessings freely bestowed. This is "the crown of righteousness, which the Lord, the righteous judge, will give me on that [last] day", the day of "his appearing" in glory.

Paul finished his testament by declaring that, in the end, the Lord would again be his rescuer "from every evil attack" and the object of Paul's praise: "To him be the glory forever and ever. Amen".

Thirty-first Sunday in Ordinary Time

God's Purpose Guides People Gently

* Wisdom 11.22–12.2
* Psalm 145
* 2 Thessalonians 1.11–2.2
* Luke 19.1-10

Today's epistle prepares us for the teaching about the end times that will begin to colour the liturgy in these closing weeks of the Church year. Meanwhile, the Book of Wisdom and Jesus' encounter with Zacchaeus tell of God's mercy to those who repent.

The Book of Wisdom was composed in Greek, late in the first century BC, at Alexandria, one of the largest centres of Diaspora Jews. The author – evidently well acquainted with Hellenistic rhetoric, philosophy and culture – wrote at a time of crisis for believers.

Many Jews had abandoned their faith for pagan religions or secular philosophies. Some combined aspects of these secular outlooks on life into a hybrid version of faith. The age-old problem of retribution – why do the wicked prosper and the virtuous suffer? – troubled people.

The wise man addressed their concerns by speaking of God's providence – divine care for creation – in prayer form. With logic he showed that God is simultaneously all-powerful and merciful: "You overlook people's sins, so that they may repent ... you would not have made anything if you had hated it ... your immortal spirit is in all things ... Therefore you correct little by little those who trespass".

God's mercy and love, he said, are proof not of weakness but of divine power. For God has a purpose in guiding people gently. Through tenderness, God warns people of the ways in which they sin so they may be "freed from wickedness and put their trust" in God.

The sage saw teaching God's mercy as a way of encouraging people to conversion. He placed personal responsibility for taking the path of repentance squarely on the shoulders of all who contemplate God's care for the world.

Jericho, the 'City of Palms', was the last stopping-off spot before people began the long, steep ascent to Jerusalem. So when Jesus reached Jericho, attentive gospel readers (and hearers) would know his journey was ending.

Jericho served as a demarcation post, as it does today between Israel and the Palestinian Authority. Near Jericho, the people of Israel had entered the Promised Land under an earlier *Yeshua* (Joshua 1–6). Though translated differently, "Joshua" and "Jesus" are variations of the same Hebrew name, meaning "God saves".

Jericho's border status made it a place for toll collectors. One of them – a head tax collector – features prominently in today's gospel.

Luke focuses on the inner dynamic of Jesus' meeting with Zacchaeus, short for "Zachariah", meaning "the righteous one". Manifestly, Zacchaeus did not live up to his name until Jesus went to stay at his house. Small of stature, Zacchaeus did not let his height impede his desire to see Jesus, but climbed a sycamore tree to see him passing by. And with joyful abandon, he accepted Jesus' decision to stay at his house.

Jericho near the Jordan serves as a biblical icon of the "salvation" God yearns to give to sinners. Such salvation was the outcome of Jesus' encounter with Zacchaeus ("Today salvation has come to this house … For the Son of Man came to seek out and to save the lost").

Zacchaeus' change of heart, proven by promises made to Jesus, of restitution and sacrificial giving to the poor, indicates the wise way in which Jesus implemented God's gentleness towards sinners.

Both Thessalonian epistles reveal Paul's advice about what must happen in the end days. Although they differ from each other in the details given, the second echoes the structure and language of the first. Plausibly, then, Second Thessalonians contains Paul's take on issues not mentioned in First Thessalonians or his correction of misinterpretations of things he had said in the earlier letter about "the coming of our Lord Jesus Christ and our being gathered together to him".

Paul reassured the Thessalonian Christians that, while Christ's end-time rule has already begun, it has not yet come to be in all its fullness (note his reference to the false belief "that the day of the Lord is already here").

God's purpose is that, through Jesus, all may ultimately share in the kingdom, once Christ has won the final victory over the enemies of his Church – even death itself. This is the consoling message of Second Thessalonians and of other scriptural readings in these last weeks of the liturgical year.

Thirty-second Sunday in Ordinary Time

The Nature of Life with God in Heaven

* 2 Maccabees 7.1-2, 7, 9-14
* Psalm 17
* 2 Thessalonians 2.16–3.5
* Luke 20.27-38

The Books of the Maccabees are deuterocanonical writings that narrate what happened in Israel during the systematic attempt by King Antiochus IV Epiphanes of Syria to suppress the Jewish religion (around 167 BC).

Under Antiochus' program, copies of the Jewish law were burned and its customs banned. Distinctively Jewish practices such as circumcision were forbidden under penalty of death. Jewish temple worship was done away with and a pagan altar erected in its place in Jerusalem.

The stories of Second Maccabees contain heartfelt and emotional appeals meant to stir up in faithful Jews dedication to observing God's commandments.

The first of seven sons presented a holy view of martyrdom ("we are ready to die rather than transgress the laws of our ancestors").

The second expressed a hope in resurrection as a reward for fidelity to God ("the King of the universe will raise us up to an everlasting renewal of life"). Who would be worthy to be raised and how resurrection would take place were questions not clearly resolved as Israelite faith developed.

The third son expressed his conviction that his loss of limbs (his hands) or members of his body (his tongue) did not matter, for he would regain these in his risen state ("I got these from Heaven ... and from God I hope to get them back again"). Conceptions of the afterlife imagined a resurrection of both good and wicked people, the former to glory and the latter to reprobation. Addressing the king, the fourth son expressed the opposite view: that his persecutors would not share in resurrection ("for you, there will be no resurrection to life!").

Not all Jews accepted the new doctrine about resurrection. Sadducees "who say there is no resurrection", held to the earlier view that the dead continued a kind of shadowy existence in the underworld called Sheol (sometimes referred to as Hades). This derived from their view that only the five books of Moses were normative for Jewish belief.

Noting that he taught the resurrection, some Sadducees tried to depict Jesus' views as foolish. They put to him a conundrum: Which of seven brothers would have as his wife at the resurrection a woman who had been married to all seven?

Before believing Israel came to understand God's power to raise the dead and accept the resurrection, people were thought to live on in their descendants. So, if a man died without children, his brother was obliged to take his wife and have children by her; this also ensured the handing on of property within the immediate family. *Levir*, the Latin word for brother-in-law, led to this practice being designated as "levirate" marriage (spelled out in Deuteronomy 25.5).

Six brothers had followed the practice of levirate marriage, attempting to secure the posterity of their deceased brother by marrying the widow and begetting a son. All, however, ended up childless.

The Sadducees imagined that relationships in heaven would continue as they had on earth. Quoting the Pentateuch, which the Sadducees recognized, Jesus challenged their reading of Scripture. He taught that in the risen life, relationships change. Families are no longer necessary in the family of God. For the "children of the resurrection" no longer need to worry about continuing the family tree. So, there is no marriage in the afterlife.

Again differing with the Sadducees, who denied the world of spirits, Jesus taught that human beings will one day take on a full spiritual existence. In the resurrection, people "are like Angels and are sons and daughters of God". Jesus said marriage was for this world only ("in the resurrection from the dead, [people] neither marry nor are given in marriage"). And "they are like Angels" – not because they do not marry, but because they do not die.

Jesus' teaching about no marriage in heaven might seem liberating to those whose earthly marriage failed or was abusive, but disappointing to those who have known lifelong marital intimacy and companionship.

One conclusion, then, is that heaven – the world to come – will surprise even believers. Still, God, who created the goodness of human life and love, including marriage, will provide life beyond death for those who have developed a capacity to love and be loved, for all those able to respond to God's love.

Thirty-third Sunday in Ordinary Time

Christ Will Come Again!

* Malachi 4.1-2
* Psalm 98
* 2 Thessalonians 3.7-12
* Luke 21.5-19

The readings at the end of one Church year and the beginning of another focus on the Parousia, the return of Jesus in glory. Christian reflection and prayer concentrate on the third element in the believing community's acclamation of faith, commonly used before the revision of the Roman Missal: "Christ has died, Christ is risen, *Christ will come again!*"

Today's gospel passage is the first half of Jesus' final address at the close of his public ministry. It is *eschatological* in nature, telling about the final phase of the world's future, the 'end times', the 'last things'.

Jesus' discourse encourages disciples, reminding them that "by your endurance you will gain your souls". The whole unit closes with a warning that is also a charge: "Be alert at all times, praying that you may have the strength to escape all these things that will take place, and to stand before the Son of Man" (21.36).

"All these things that will take place" evokes a scenario about the end of the world that seems frightening, especially nowadays. People may feel that the imagery ("wars and insurrections ... famines and plagues ... dreadful portents and great signs from heaven") bears chilling parallels to what the world has been experiencing since the terrorist attacks of September 11, 2001.

For like the speeches found in Mark 13 and Matthew chapters 24 and 25, Jesus makes use of *apocalyptic* language to communicate gospel truths. His speech 'uncovers' or 'reveals' – for that is the meaning of the noun "apocalypse" and the adjective "apocalyptic" – God's designs for his chosen ones, the disciples of Jesus and members of his Church.

The purpose of all apocalyptic language, which is strongly dualistic, with stark contrasts between good and evil, is to encourage the faithful by revealing God's plan. The present evil order soon will be overcome and God's victory and vindication enacted.

It is important, however, to realize that, since the future of the world's salvation remains hidden in God's sovereign wisdom, even what is revealed cannot now be fully understood by human beings. Faith in God and trust in his saving designs are called for in order to correctly interpret Jesus' prophecies about the future.

Jesus urged his disciples to a patient endurance, rooted in faith, love and hope. They are not to be frightened or led astray, but assured that – in whatever persecution may come – Jesus will give them an eloquence and wisdom that their enemies will be unable to resist or contradict. They may be confident about what is to come because he remains the Lord of History.

The Book of Malachi, a prophecy whose title means 'my messenger', embodies God's promise of an end-time figure who would "prepare the way" for God's renewal of Israel's faith life. The anonymous author of these oracles lived in Judah two generations after the people of God had come back from exile in Babylon (about 460 BC).

Though the Temple had been rebuilt, it was a sorry sight. The twenty thousand returned exiles were poor and without material resources to rebuild the Temple. As well, they had grown weary in religious practice. Jews divorced the "wives of their youth" to marry pretty foreign women (Malachi 2.14). The wealthy not only cheated the poor, they even sold them into slavery (3.5).

The prophet's oracles are a kind of catechism, laying out convictions about God's special love for Israel, the sins of the priests, God's opposition to divorce, God's love of justice, criticism of ritual offenses, and assurance of the coming triumph of the just.

Malachi's vision said that the world could soon confidently look forward to a day when the least shadow of evil would be blotted out, in effect heralding Jesus' prophecy.

The issue underlying Second Thessalonians seems clear enough. Some disciples had become so caught up in speculation about the end times and talk of the nearness of Jesus' return that they withdrew from daily duties of life (work, family commitments, etc.) under the pretext that "the day of the Lord is already here" (2.3).

Paul offered his own way of life as a model to be imitated in how to live in expectation of the end: doing hard work, not being a burden to anyone, not interfering with another's work. Every Christian was to support himself or herself. While zealously longing for Jesus' glorious return, the Christian is to engage fully in his or her earthly tasks and commitments.

Thirty-fourth Sunday in Ordinary Time

Christ the King

Living in the Kingdom of God's Son

* 2 Samuel 5.1-3
* Psalm 122
* Colossians 1.12-20
* Luke 23.35-43

The Second Book of Kings tells of David's designation as king over all Israel, the union of northern tribes (Israel) with the southern kingdom (Judah) under his leadership.

Israelite motivation for their choice of David as "shepherd" and "ruler" lay in his military leadership and God's decision to take the throne from Saul and entrust it to David (cf. 2 Samuel 3.10).

David was depicted as a pastoral ruler leading by persuasion. But Israel's union was only surface-deep. Underneath, internal conflicts raged, ready to boil over at any time – as David's 33-year rule showed. True and lasting kingship would await another "anointed one" in David's lineage.

In the gospel, Jesus exercises his rule as God's anointed with kingly right to open the doors of Paradise to those who come into fellowship with him.

Luke's depiction of the crucifixion shows three negative responses to the Crucified balanced by three positive responses, including one offered by the so-called good thief.

Those humiliating Jesus were the religious leaders, the soldiers and a criminal. The positive dispositions towards him came, in reverse order, from a criminal and – beyond today's gospel reading – from a centurion and the people (cf. 23.46-48).

The catcalls tempted Jesus to hang on to his life ("let him save himself"; "save yourself"; "save yourself and us!" as well), a stance completely at odds with his teaching about the true way to life (cf. 9.24).

LIVING GOD'S WORD - YEAR C

Jesus' fate on the Cross embodied that of the world's marginalized in every age: "scoffed at", "mocked", "derided" and "rebuked". Jesus accepted it all with serenity and inner peace, or so it seemed to one of the criminals crucified with him.

Inwardly, this became a moment of grace for him. He responded by defending Jesus' innocence to the abusive criminal, admitting his own guilt and asking Jesus to "remember me when you come into your kingdom".

The meaning of "remember" has been interpreted as asking for a share in the mercy that only a king can give. Perhaps the criminal was conscious that, because of his deeds, his personal fate would differ from the one awaiting Jesus. Or perhaps he knew that he could do nothing now to merit God's favour.

Whatever his intention, the criminal's gesture of humility moved Jesus – as often happened during his ministry – to reach out with comfort and a saving word. As St. Ambrose put it, "More abundant is the favour shown than the request made".

Christ the king, ruling on the Cross, offered salvation to one who unexpectedly repented. The generalized "when" of the criminal's petition became "today" in Jesus' assurance that "you will be with me in Paradise". The day of his crucifixion became the day of the criminal's entry into Paradise.

The word "today" on Jesus' lips echoes its frequent use elsewhere in the Gospel, showing that in him the era of salvation has become a reality for the world (cf. 2.11; 4.21; 5.26; 19.11).

"Paradise" is a Persian loan-word meaning "garden" or "park" and, though having secular connotations, was used to refer to the Garden of Eden (cf. Isaiah 51.3). It came to symbolize the future bliss of God's people.

In 2 Corinthians 12.4 and Revelation 2.7, Paradise symbolizes heaven and its happiness. It is the realm where Jesus exercises his kingly rule. In Christian thought, Paradise became known as the intermediate resting place for the souls of the righteous dead.

Colossae was located in the Lycus Valley, in today's southwestern Turkey. In the mid-first century, a Christian community existed there, perhaps founded by Epaphras (Colossians 1.7-8). The precipitating cause of the letter, written by Paul or possibly a disciple, was the appearance of a philosophy or tradition that was troubling because it suggested that Christ was not all-sufficient to the spiritual needs of the Colossians.

The precise nature of the Colossian heresy has been much debated: some were demanding circumcision (2.11), the keeping of Sabbaths, new moons, festivals and dietary restrictions. But the inspired author insists that men and women have no need to retreat from the world into some esoteric cult or practice to live good and upright lives. Here and now they have the power, from Christ and through their baptism, to live a high degree of morality. This is what it means to live in the kingdom of God's Son.